THE THREE LOOPS THAT RUN YOUR LIFE

WHY YOU'RE STUCK, BURNT OUT, OR EMPTY — AND THE SYSTEM YOU'RE ALREADY RUNNING

A SYSTEMS MANUAL FOR WHY SMART PEOPLE STILL GET STUCK — AND WHAT ACTUALLY CHANGES IT

LEE POWELL

PREFACE

"Most suffering isn't character failure. It's structural confusion."

Most people are not lost because they lack insight.

They are lost because they are running the wrong loop for the problem they are in.

This distinction matters more than almost anything else in the self-improvement conversation. It explains why smart people stay stuck. Why therapy stalls. Why spiritual practice floats above daily life without changing it. Why ambitious people burn out while lazy people stagnate. Why the same patterns repeat for decades despite genuine effort to break them.

The problem isn't intelligence. It isn't willpower. It isn't trauma, though trauma complicates things. It isn't laziness or moral failure or some deficiency of character that needs to be fixed.

The problem is structural. And structural problems require structural solutions.

Modern culture has collapsed three fundamentally different human processes into one blurry instruction set.

Heal yourself. Grow yourself. Find your purpose.

These directives float around interchangeably, as if they're variations on the same theme. They're not. They refer to different systems. They obey different rules. They require different actions. They break in different ways.

Treating them as interchangeable is like treating the foundation, the walls, and the roof of a building as the same thing. They're all part of the structure. They're not the same structure. And if you try to install a roof while your foundation is cracked, the building falls down.

This is what happens to people. They try to find purpose while their self-trust is shattered. They try to grow while their foundation is broken. They try to serve while they're falling apart. The effort is real. The sequence is wrong. The result is collapse, confusion, or quiet desperation that never quite resolves.

This book exists because most suffering is not what people think it is.

It's not moral failure. Most people who are stuck are not bad people making bad choices. They're decent people applying effort in the wrong direction.

It's not trauma — at least not always. Trauma is real and requires specific intervention. But many people who are stuck don't have significant trauma. They have structural confusion. They're running systems incorrectly, not carrying wounds that need healing.

It's not lack of effort. The people who pick up books like this are usually trying. Often trying hard. Often exhausted from trying. The effort isn't the problem. The direction is.

What most suffering is: loop confusion. Running the wrong system for the problem at hand. Applying growth when what's needed is stabilisation. Seeking meaning when what's needed is capability. Trying to heal what isn't wounded while ignoring the structure that's broken.

This confusion isn't personal failure. It's the natural result of never having seen the machinery clearly. No one showed you how human lives operate. No one explained the systems, the sequence, the failure modes. You were given vague instructions — be better, try harder, find yourself — without any structural understanding of what those instructions mean or how to execute them.

This book provides that structure.

There are three loops that govern human functioning.

The first is the Self-Trust Loop. It determines whether you believe your own word. Whether promises you make to yourself mean anything. Whether your system invests in your intentions or dismisses them before you begin.

The second is the Growth Loop. It determines whether you develop capability, strength, competence. Whether you can enter discomfort and emerge more capable. Whether your capacity expands or stagnates.

The third is the Meaning Loop. It determines whether your effort connects to something beyond yourself. Whether the work sustains itself over time. Whether you have an answer to the question that survival and success never touch: why bother?

These loops are always running. You're running them right now. You were running them before you picked up this book, and you'll run them until you die. The question isn't whether to engage them. The question is whether you'll engage them consciously or let them run by default.

Default is what got most people where they are. Default is the confusion, the misdirection, the decades of effort that never lands. Default is running yesterday's loop for today's problem, over and over, wondering why nothing changes.

Conscious engagement is different. It requires seeing the machinery. Understanding the sequence. Knowing which loop needs attention and providing it. Knowing when to stabilize, when to push, when to serve, and when to stop.

That's what this book teaches.

A note on what this book is not.

It is not a self-help book in the conventional sense. Self-help typically offers motivation, encouragement, and vague directives to become a better version of yourself. This book offers machinery. How the systems work. What breaks them. What repairs them. Motivation is irrelevant if you're running the wrong loop. Encouragement doesn't help if the structure is wrong.

It is not a therapy book. Therapy has its place — this book has an entire chapter on when therapy is necessary and this book isn't enough. But therapy often operates in a different domain: processing emotion, healing wounds, understanding the past. This book operates in the domain of structure: feedback systems, sequences, operational repair. The domains can complement each other. They're not the same domain.

It is not a spirituality book. Meaning is addressed here, but not as transcendence or enlightenment or connection to something cosmic. Meaning is addressed as a feedback loop — a system that either runs properly or doesn't, that either produces the experience of mattering or produces emptiness and nihilism. The mechanics are what matter. The metaphysics are irrelevant.

It is not a productivity book. Productivity books typically offer tactics for doing more, faster, better. This book offers something different: understanding which system you should be running in the first place. All the productivity tactics in the world don't help if you're optimizing the wrong thing. Getting more efficient at the wrong loop accelerates the dysfunction.

It is not a book for men specifically, though men will recognize themselves immediately. The loops are human loops. They operate the same way regardless of gender. The examples throughout are drawn from human experience broadly, not male experience specifically. Women who are tired of emotional labour framing, who want structural explanation than psychologized interpretation, will find what they're looking for here.

A note on what this book requires.

It requires honesty. The loops don't respond to self-deception. They respond to reality — to what you do, not what you intend or wish or believe about yourself. Diagnosing which loop is broken requires honest assessment. Repairing a loop requires honest engagement. The comfort of flattering self-narratives has to be sacrificed for the utility of accurate ones.

It requires patience. The loops don't repair overnight. The foundation takes time to rebuild. Growth regulation takes time to establish. Meaning takes time to earn. The person who wants transformation by next Tuesday will be disappointed. The person who builds slowly, consistently, over months and years, will get everything.

It requires action. Understanding the loops is not the same as running them properly. Insight doesn't change anything — that's one of the core arguments of this book. The loops update through action, through kept promises, through deliberate discomfort, through contribution. Reading is not repair. The book can show you the machinery. You have to run it.

It requires acceptance. Acceptance that the loops exist whether you like them or not. That you're subject to feedback systems you didn't choose. That the question isn't whether to play the game but how to play it well. Resistance to this reality doesn't change the reality. It makes the dysfunction more persistent.

What this book offers.

Clarity about the machinery. The three loops, how they work, how they break, how they interact. A structural understanding of human functioning that explains patterns you've observed but couldn't articulate.

Diagnostic precision. The ability to look at your current condition and identify which loop is broken — not which loop you'd prefer to work on, not which loop sounds most interesting, but which loop is the source of your current dysfunction.

Repair protocols. Specific interventions for each loop. Not vague advice to "work on yourself" but concrete practices that address specific failure modes. What to do when self-trust is broken. What to do when growth is dysregulated. What to do when meaning is starved or premature.

The skill of loop switching. Knowing which loop to run today. When to stabilize, when to push, when to serve, when to stop. The adult skill that no one teaches but everyone needs.

And most importantly: a different relationship with your own stuckness. Not as moral failure. Not as character flaw. Not as evidence that something is fundamentally wrong with you. As structural confusion that can be diagnosed and addressed. As machinery running incorrectly that can be adjusted.

That reframe alone changes things. The shame dissolves when you realize the problem is structural, not personal. The path forward clarifies when you can see which system needs attention. The effort becomes productive when it's pointed in the right direction.

The loops are already running.

They were running before you knew they existed. They'll keep running whether you engage with this book or not. The machinery operates regardless of your awareness of it.

But awareness changes what's possible. Seeing the structure lets you work with it instead of against it. Understanding the sequence lets you build properly instead of randomly. Knowing the failure modes lets you catch problems before they cascade.

This book is a manual for machinery you're already operating. It doesn't give you new equipment. It shows you how to use what you have.

The rest is up to you.

What you do with the clarity — whether you engage the repair protocols, build the foundation, direct your growth, earn the meaning — that's yours to decide. The book can illuminate. It cannot act for you.

But at least now you can see.

The loops are running. The machinery is visible. The structure is clear.

Now the work begins.

HOW TO USE THIS BOOK

"Reading is not repair. The loops update through action, not understanding."

This book is organized as a sequence, not a menu.

That matters because most people read self-improvement books wrong. They skim for the parts that seem relevant. They jump to the chapter that matches their self-diagnosis. They extract tactics without understanding the system those tactics belong to.

This approach fails here. The loops depend on each other. The sequence matters. Skipping to Loop 3 because meaning sounds more interesting than self-trust will produce the same confusion that got you stuck in the first place.

Read the book in order. At least the first time.

The structure follows a specific logic.

Part I explains the machinery. What feedback loops are, why they govern human functioning, and why insight alone doesn't change them. This isn't background material you can skip. It's the foundation for everything that follows. If you don't understand why the loops matter, the repair protocols won't make sense.

Part II presents the three loops in detail. Each loop gets its own chapter: what it governs, how it works mechanically, how it fails, what the failure signatures look like. These chapters are the core of the book. They give you the language to see patterns you've been living but couldn't name.

Part III addresses diagnosis. How to determine which loop is broken in your situation. This is harder than it sounds. Humans compensate for broken loops with other loops, which obscures the real problem.[1] This section teaches you to see through the compensation to the actual structural failure.

Part IV provides repair protocols. Specific interventions for each loop. Not generic advice — loop-specific practices designed to address the particular failure mode you're dealing with. This is where reading turns into action.

Part V teaches loop switching. The skill of knowing which loop to run in which situation. This is the integration — taking what you've learned about each loop and applying it dynamically to the changing conditions of your life.

Part VI maps the loops across a lifetime. How the loops express differently at different ages. What's demanded at twenty-five versus forty-five versus sixty-five. The mistakes that are common at each stage and what helps.

Part VII addresses limits. When this book isn't enough. When professional help is needed. How to seek it without shame. This chapter exists because structural repair has boundaries, and knowing those boundaries is part of using the model responsibly.

The final chapter describes what coherence looks like. Not as an ideal to aspire to, but as a concrete picture of what happens when the loops run well. What it feels like to live without the internal war that broken loops produce.

A note on diagnosis.

Most people misdiagnose themselves.

They think they have a meaning problem when they have a self-trust problem. They think they need more growth when they need to regulate the growth they have. They think they're lazy when they're running a broken feedback system that's stopped investing in their intentions.

The misdiagnosis isn't stupidity. It's the natural result of loop confusion. When you can't see the loops, you can't accurately identify which one is broken. You reach for explanations that feel true but miss the structural reality.

This book will challenge your self-diagnosis. You might be convinced you know what's wrong. The diagnostic chapters might suggest something different. When that happens, resist the urge to dismiss the new diagnosis in favor of the familiar one.

The familiar diagnosis is what you've been working with. It hasn't fixed the problem. Maybe the problem is different than you thought.

A note on action.

Reading this book will not change you.

Understanding the loops will not repair them. Recognizing your failure mode will not correct it. Seeing the pattern clearly will not dissolve it.

This is the central argument of Chapter 2, and it applies to this book as much as to any other source of insight. The loops don't update from understanding. They update from action. From kept promises. From deliberate discomfort. From contribution.

The book provides clarity. Clarity is valuable — it tells you where to point your effort. But clarity without effort produces nothing except more sophisticated stuckness. You'll understand your dysfunction better. You'll still be dysfunctional.

The repair protocols in Part IV are meant to be done, not read. The practices are specific because vague practices don't work. They're small because small actions are what rebuild broken systems.

If you read this book and do nothing, the book has failed. Not because the model is wrong, but because you used it wrong. The model requires action. The action is yours to take.

A note on patience.

The loops didn't break overnight. They won't repair overnight.

Self-trust eroded over years of broken promises. It rebuilds over months of kept ones. Growth dysregulated through decades of unchecked achievement. It regulates through sustained practice of bounded effort. Meaning starved over a lifetime of effort disconnected from contribution. It rebuilds through consistent service over time.

The person who reads this book expecting transformation by next month will be disappointed. The repair is real, but it's gradual. The evidence accumulates slowly. The identity shifts incrementally.

This is frustrating. Everyone wants fast results. But fast results in loop repair are an illusion. What looks like fast change is usually compensation — switching to a different dysfunction that temporarily feels better. Real repair takes time because the systems that need repairing are deep, and deep systems don't shift quickly.

Expect months, not weeks. Expect gradual improvement, not dramatic transformation. Expect setbacks that don't erase progress but do test patience. That's what real repair looks like.

A note on sequence.

If multiple loops are broken — and for many people, they are — the repair sequence matters.

Loop 1 first. Always. The foundation has to be stable before growth can be regulated or meaning can be built. You can't keep promises to what you serve if you can't keep promises to yourself. You can't sustain deliberate discomfort if your system doesn't believe you'll follow through.

This will feel wrong to some readers. Loop 1 work is unglamorous. Small promises, visible evidence, slow accumulation of trust. It doesn't feel like the important work. It feels like preliminary work, like something to get through before the real stuff.

That feeling is part of why the foundation broke in the first place. The same impatience that skipped over self-trust in favor of achievement or meaning will want to skip over it again now. The desire to jump to the interesting loops is the pattern that needs to be interrupted.

Start with Loop 1. Even if you think the problem is elsewhere. Especially if you think the problem is elsewhere. The foundation is where you build from. Everything else is built on sand until the foundation is solid.

A note on honesty.

The book will be useful to the degree that you're honest with yourself while reading it.

The diagnostic questions require honest answers. Not the answers that make you look good, not the answers you wish were true, not the answers that protect your self-image. The actual answers. What's happening in your life. Which patterns are present.

This is harder than it sounds. Humans are skilled at self-deception. The same mechanisms that produce loop confusion produce confusion about the confusion. You can read the description of broken self-trust and think "that's not me" while exhibiting every symptom on the list.

The book can't force honesty. It can only invite it. What you do with the invitation is up to you.

But know this: the loops don't respond to the story you tell about yourself. They respond to reality. Deceive yourself about which loop is broken, and the repair efforts will be misdirected. Admit which loop is broken, and the repair can begin.

The discomfort of honest self-assessment is the price of repair. There's no way around it.

A note on judgment.

This book describes failure modes without moralizing about them.

Broken self-trust isn't a character flaw. It's a feedback system that's been trained, through repeated experience, to stop investing in your intentions. Dysregulated growth isn't a moral failing. It's a loop that's been running without boundaries, doing what loops do when they're not constrained. Starved meaning isn't spiritual inadequacy. It's a system that hasn't been fed what it needs.

These are structural descriptions, not judgments. The language is mechanical because the reality is mechanical. The loops don't care about your worth as a person. They run according to the inputs they receive.

If you find yourself feeling judged while reading the failure mode descriptions, notice that. The judgment is coming from you, not from the book. The book is describing what happens. The shame or self-criticism you add on top is extra — and it's not useful.

Shame doesn't repair loops. It makes repair harder. The energy spent on self-judgment is energy not spent on action. The correct response to recognizing a broken loop isn't to feel bad about it. It's to repair it.

A note on limits.

This book has boundaries.

It addresses structural dysfunction — loops running incorrectly that can be reconfigured through deliberate practice. It doesn't address pathology — conditions that require clinical intervention, medication, or specialized treatment.

Chapter 16 addresses this directly. But it's worth noting here: if you recognize yourself in that chapter more than in the repair protocols, the book is telling you something. The structural model has limits. Some problems exceed those limits. Knowing which side of the line you're on is part of using the book responsibly.

Professional help isn't failure. It's using the right tool. A screwdriver isn't ashamed that it can't hammer nails. It's the wrong tool for that job. This book is a tool. It works for certain problems. For other problems, you need different tools.

What success looks like.

If you use this book correctly, here's what happens:

You start noticing loops. Not as abstract concepts, but as patterns operating in your actual life. You notice when self-trust is eroding. You notice when growth is consuming than serving. You notice when meaning is starved or premature.

You get better at calling the real problem. When something feels wrong, you can identify which system is misfiring. Not the surface symptom — the structural cause. This changes everything about how you approach problems.

You develop repair capacity. You know what to do when each loop breaks. Not vague advice to "work on it" — specific practices that address specific failures. The repair becomes something you can execute, not understand.

You develop switching skill. You know which loop to run in which conditions. When to stabilize, when to push, when to serve, when to stop. The adult skill that no one teaches becomes something you can do.

And underneath all of it: you develop a different relationship with your own stuckness. Not as evidence of personal failure. As structural confusion that you now have tools to address.

That's what success looks like. Not perfection. Not permanent resolution. The ability to see the machinery, diagnose accurately, repair what's broken, and run the right loop for the situation you're in.

That's what this book offers.

The system is already live.

They were running before you opened this book. They'll keep running as you read it. The machinery doesn't wait for your understanding. It operates whether you see it or not.

But now you're going to see it.

Turn the page. Let's look at the first loop.

PART ONE
THE INVISIBLE MACHINERY

CHAPTER 1
YOU'RE ALREADY RUNNING LOOPS

"Confidence, motivation, and meaning are effects, not causes. The loops produce them—or don't."

Something is running your life. It's been running for years.

You didn't design it. You didn't choose it. Most days, you don't even notice it. But it's there — underneath your decisions, behind your moods, shaping what you attempt and what you avoid.

It's not your personality. It's not your trauma. It's not your zodiac sign or your childhood attachment style or whatever label the last book pinned on you.

It's a system. Three interlocking feedback loops that govern whether you trust yourself, whether you grow, and whether your effort ever turns into meaning.

When these loops run cleanly, life feels coherent. Not easy. Not happy. Coherent. You do what you say you'll do. You improve where improvement matters. You contribute in ways that don't hollow you out.

When these loops are confused — when you're running the

wrong one for the problem you're in — everything starts to break. Slowly at first. Then all at once.

Here's how a feedback loop works.

You take an action. Reality responds. Your system updates based on that response. The update shapes your next action.

This isn't metaphor. It's how you learned to walk. To speak. To stop touching things that hurt. Every capability you have was built through this cycle: action, feedback, update, action.

The brain doesn't learn from ideas. It learns from consequences.[1] You can understand something perfectly and still be unable to do it, because understanding happens in language while learning happens in loops.[2]

This is why insight fails. Why therapy can stall. Why you can read a hundred books about discipline and still negotiate with yourself every morning about whether to get out of bed.

The knowing part of you operates in one system. The doing part operates in another. And the doing part doesn't care what the knowing part thinks.

Consider what happens when you make a promise to yourself. Say you commit to waking up earlier. You set the alarm. You tell yourself this time will be different. You mean it.

Then the alarm goes off. And the negotiation begins. Five more minutes. I'll start tomorrow. I didn't sleep well. The loop registers all of this. Not the intention — the behavior. Not what you meant — what you did.

Do this enough times, and the system stops believing the alarm means anything. The intention becomes noise. The promise becomes irrelevant. This isn't a willpower problem. It's a credibility problem.[3] You've trained your own system not to take you seriously.

This is happening constantly, in every domain. Every time you say "I should" and don't follow through. Every time you plan and don't execute. Every time you know exactly what to do and watch yourself not do it.

The loop is updating. The pattern is strengthening. And no amount of insight will reverse it.

Most of what you call "psychology" — confidence, motivation, discipline, burnout, shame — these aren't root causes. They're symptoms. Secondary effects of loop function.

Confidence isn't something you build directly. It's the residue of a loop that's working — action producing evidence that updates identity in a favorable direction.

Motivation isn't a resource you can stockpile. It's a signal that the system believes you. When motivation vanishes, it's not because you're lazy. It's because somewhere in the loop, trust has broken down.

Shame isn't a character flaw. It's a diagnostic signal. The system is registering a gap between what you say you are and what the evidence shows.

Burnout isn't working too hard. It's running the wrong loop for too long, demanding growth when what's needed is stabilization, or pushing for meaning when the foundation isn't there.

None of this gets fixed by understanding. It gets fixed by identifying which loop is broken and running the correct repair sequence.

There are three loops.

They're always running. You're running them right now. You were running them before you picked up this book, and you'll be running them after you put it down.

The question isn't whether you're running them. The question is whether you're running them well.

The first loop is Self-Trust.

Action → Evidence → Identity → Action.

This loop determines whether you believe your own word. It's the foundation. When it's working, you do what you say you'll do, the evidence accumulates, and your identity stabilizes around someone who can be relied upon — by yourself.

This loop operates below language. It doesn't care about your reasons, your justifications, or your intentions. It only records what you do. Miss a commitment, and the loop adjusts your identity downward. Keep a commitment, and it adjusts upward. The process is automatic. It's been running since you were a child.

When it breaks, you enter a condition that looks like many things — procrastination, lack of motivation, chronic planning, "I know what I should do but..." syndrome. What it is: the system no longer believes your promises. So it stops investing in them.

The second loop is Growth.

Discomfort → Skill → Capacity → Higher Standard → Discomfort.

This loop determines whether you improve. You enter deliberate discomfort. You acquire skill. Your capacity increases. Your standards rise. You seek the next edge.

This is the loop of learning, earning, building, becoming capable. It runs on effort and produces competence. It's the loop that built your career, your skills, your ability to navigate complexity.

When it's working, you get stronger, more capable, more competent. When it breaks — either by over-identification (you become your output) or by avoidance (you spiritualize stagnation) — the loop either consumes you or abandons you. Over-identification looks like burnout, brittle ego, and the terror of not performing. Avoidance looks like comfort disguised as enlightenment, anti-ambition masquerading as wisdom.

The third loop is Meaning.

Service → Impact → Significance → Responsibility → Service.

This loop determines whether your effort sustains itself over time. You contribute beyond yourself. Impact is felt. Significance emerges. Responsibility expands. You serve again, deeper.

This is the loop that answers the question survival doesn't answer: Why bother? Once you're fed, housed, and safe, what's the point of continued effort? Loop 3 answers that question. Not with philosophy. With structure.

When it's working, effort feels worthwhile even when it's hard. When it breaks — either by premature activation (trying to serve while unstable) or by starvation (all growth, no contribution) — you get either martyrdom or nihilism.[4] Premature meaning looks like boundary collapse, over-giving, saving the world while your own life falls apart. Meaning starvation looks like cynicism, emptiness, success that tastes like nothing.

These loops are not sequential forever. You don't complete Loop 1, then graduate to Loop 2, then arrive at Loop 3.

They're hierarchical but concurrent.

All three are always running. But they have a dependency structure. Loop 2 functions poorly without Loop 1. Loop 3 functions poorly without Loops 1 and 2.

This is where most people go wrong.

They try to find meaning while their self-trust is shattered. The meaning collapses under the weight of their own unreliability.

They try to grow while their foundation is broken. The growth produces achievement without stability — impressive scaffolding around an empty building.

They try to serve while they're falling apart. The service becomes martyrdom, or it becomes manipulation disguised as generosity.

The hierarchy isn't about moral development. It's about structural integrity. You can't build the second floor if the first floor is cracked.

· · ·

Most suffering isn't trauma. It isn't failure. It isn't bad luck.

Most suffering is loop confusion.

Running the Growth loop when what's needed is Self-Trust repair.

Running the Meaning loop when what's needed is Growth.

Compensating with one loop because another feels too hard to fix.

This is what the self-help industry misses. It treats symptoms — the lack of motivation, the burnout, the emptiness — without diagnosing the structural cause. It prescribes habits for people whose habit-keeping machinery is broken. It offers purpose to people who can't yet be trusted to show up for themselves. It pushes growth on people who are already drowning in it.

The successful person who feels hollow? They mastered Loop 2 and starved Loop 3. Decades of achievement, nothing to show for it internally. The spiritual person who feels ineffective? They're oriented toward Loop 3 without having stabilized Loop 1. All the meaning in the world, but no foundation to carry it. The driven person who can't stop? Loop 2 has become a substitute for identity than an expression of it. They don't work to grow. They work to avoid the quiet.

The person who helps everyone but themselves? Loop 3 running without Loop 1. Service as avoidance. Generosity as self-abandonment.

The person who plans endlessly but executes nothing? Loop 1 is so broken that the system won't even fund the first step. Not laziness. Not fear. Just a rational response to a credibility collapse.

Every pattern of stuckness maps to a loop problem. Not a character problem. Not a willpower problem. A structural problem.

And structural problems require structural solutions.

Here's what this book will not do.

Motivation isn't a resource. It's a signal. When it's absent, the system has stopped believing you.

It won't motivate you. Motivation is a signal from the loop system. Until the loops are addressed, motivation is irrelevant.

It won't heal you. Healing is the wrong frame. Machines aren't healed. They're diagnosed, repaired, and recalibrated.

It won't give you meaning. Meaning isn't given. It's earned through a functioning Loop 3, which requires functioning Loops 1 and 2.

It won't make you feel better about yourself. Feeling better is a byproduct of loops running cleanly. Pursue the feeling directly and you'll produce the opposite.

Here's what this book will do.

It will show you the machinery. The invisible structure that's been running underneath your decisions, your moods, your failures, and your successes.

It will give you a diagnostic frame. A way to look at your current condition and ask the right question: Which loop is broken? Not "what's wrong with me" — but "which system is misfiring, and why?"

It will give you repair protocols. Not generic advice. Loop-specific interventions that address the actual failure mode you're in.

It will teach you loop switching. The adult skill no one teaches: knowing when to stabilize, when to push, when to serve, and when to stop.

And it will do this without flattering you, without reassuring you, and without pretending that reading a book is the same as doing the work.

Understanding is not change. Reading is not repair. The loops don't update from insight. They update from action.

But action without direction is movement. And most people are moving constantly without going anywhere.

. . .

You picked up this book for a reason.

Maybe you're stuck. The same patterns, the same failures, the same morning negotiations with yourself. You know what to do. You've known for years. And still, nothing moves.

Maybe you're burnt out. You did everything right. You built the career, hit the targets, accumulated the evidence of success. And none of it feels like anything.

Maybe you're lost. Not in crisis, exactly. Just... uncertain what any of it is for. Going through the motions without the sense that the motions matter.

Each of these is a loop problem. A specific, identifiable, addressable loop problem.

The stuck pattern is almost always Loop 1 — Self-Trust. The system no longer believes you'll follow through. So it stops funding your intentions.

The burnt-out pattern is almost always Loop 2 — Growth without regulation. You've been running the achievement loop so long it's consumed everything else. There's no identity underneath the output. Burnout isn't too much work. It's the wrong loop for too long.

The lost pattern is almost always Loop 3 — Meaning starvation. You've built capacity without direction. The engine is powerful and has nowhere to go.

None of these require motivation. None of them require willpower. None of them require becoming a different person.

They require running the correct loop for the problem you're in.

The loops are always running.

They were running before you understood them. They'll keep running whether you engage with this book or not.

The only question is whether they run by default or by design.

Default is what got you here. Default is the pattern you've been repeating, the stuckness that persists, the exhaustion that doesn't resolve.

Design is different. Design is seeing the machinery clearly enough to intervene where intervention matters. To stabilize what's broken. To grow where growth is required. To serve where service is earned.

That's what this book is for.

Not to fix you. To show you which part of the machine needs attention — and how to provide it.

This is already happening, whether you see it or not.

Now let's see what they're doing.

CHAPTER 2
WHY INSIGHT DOESN'T CHANGE ANYTHING

"You can't think your way into a new way of acting; you can only act your way into a new way of thinking." – Bill Wilson [1]

You already know what's wrong.

You've known for years. You could write the diagnosis yourself. The patterns, the tendencies, the ways you sabotage, the things you avoid. You've read the books. You've had the conversations. You've journaled until your hand cramped. You've sat in therapy and named the wounds with clinical precision.

And still, nothing changes.

Not because you're broken. Not because you lack willpower. Not because you haven't gone deep enough.

Because insight operates in the wrong system. Insight without execution is a hobby. An expensive one, but still a hobby.

Here's what happens when you understand something.

The verbal, conscious part of your brain — the part that

reads, reasons, and explains — registers a new pattern. It files the information. It makes connections. It says: "Ah, I see now."

This feels significant. It feels like progress. Sometimes it even feels like change.

But the system that governs your behavior doesn't operate in language. It operates in consequences. It learns from what you do, not what you understand. It updates from action and feedback, not from insight and explanation.

These are different systems. They run on different hardware. And the one that controls your life doesn't care what the other one thinks.

This is why you can understand exactly why you procrastinate and still procrastinate. Why you can explain your avoidance patterns fluently and still avoid. Why you can articulate your fear with perfect clarity and still be paralyzed by it.

The knowing part of you updated. The doing part didn't notice.

The brain has two broad modes of learning.

The first is declarative. This is knowledge you can state. Facts, concepts, explanations, theories. It lives in language. You can write it down, discuss it, teach it to someone else. It's what you get from books, lectures, and conversations.

The second is procedural. This is knowledge that lives in action. Skills, habits, reflexes, patterns. You can't fully articulate it. You acquired it through repetition, consequence, and feedback. It's what you get from doing, failing, adjusting, and doing again.

Insight is declarative. Loop repair is procedural.

They don't transfer automatically.

You can understand balance perfectly and still fall off a bicycle. You can explain the physics of swimming and still drown. You can describe healthy boundaries in detail and still let everyone walk over you.

Declarative knowledge does not install procedural competence. You have to build procedural competence the way it was always built — through the loop. Action, evidence, update.

Consider someone learning to drive. They can read the manual. They can understand the physics of braking distance, the mechanics of steering, the rules of the road. They can pass the written test with perfect scores.

Then they get behind the wheel and panic at the first intersection.

Because knowing how to drive and being able to drive are different things. The knowing happened through reading. The being able only happens through doing — through hours of action, feedback, adjustment, and repetition until the skill lives in the body, not the mind.

Now apply this to the patterns that run your life.

You can understand why you avoid difficult conversations. That understanding won't make you have them. You can explain your relationship to money with therapeutic precision. That explanation won't change how you behave with money. You can articulate your self-sabotage patterns better than any therapist. That articulation won't stop them.

The loop doesn't update from what you know. It updates from what you do.

Therapy stalls when it stays declarative.

This isn't an attack on therapy. Therapy can be essential. For trauma, for crisis, for patterns too tangled to see alone. Good therapy has saved lives. The problem isn't therapy itself. The problem is therapy that never leaves the room.

Here's the pattern:

You go to therapy. You talk. You uncover things. You name the wounds, trace them to their origins, understand why you are the way you are. You feel seen. You feel heard. You gain insight after insight.

The hour ends. You feel lighter. You schedule next week.

And then you leave. And nothing in your behavior changes. You go home to the same patterns, the same avoidances, the same negotiations with yourself. The insight stays in the session. The loop stays unchanged.

Because the session was declarative. You explained. You understood. You processed. But the loop that governs your daily behavior wasn't touched. The system that decides whether you trust yourself, whether you follow through, whether you show up — that system is still running the same code.

Insight without action is rehearsal. You're practicing the understanding without ever performing the change.

Some people stay in this mode for years. Decades. They become fluent in their own dysfunction. They can narrate their patterns with therapeutic precision. But the patterns persist because the loop was never engaged.

The nervous system doesn't update from conversation. It updates from consequence.

If you want therapy to work, you have to take the insight out of the room and into the loop. Do something different. Let reality respond. Let the system register new evidence. Then the update becomes real.

Spirituality floats when it skips the foundation.

This is the other trap. The insight is about meaning, purpose, connection to something larger. The feeling is transcendent. The experience is real. The retreat was profound. The meditation practice opened something.

And then you return to ordinary life and can't get out of bed.

Because meaning doesn't work without self-trust. Purpose doesn't hold without foundation. You can have the most profound spiritual insight in human history, and it will evaporate by Tuesday if Loop 1 is broken.

Spiritual bypassing is real. It looks like enlightenment but functions as avoidance. The pattern goes like this:

Loop 1 is damaged. You don't trust yourself. Your daily life is full of broken promises, unfulfilled intentions, quiet shame.

Rather than repair the foundation — which is slow, unglamorous, and requires showing up for the small things — you skip to Loop 3. You orient toward meaning, service, higher purpose. It feels better. It feels elevated. It lets you avoid the grinding work of becoming someone who keeps their word.

But meaning can't be held by someone who can't hold themselves. The structure collapses. The purpose feels hollow. The insight that seemed so powerful becomes another failed promise.

This is why some of the most "spiritually advanced" people can't manage their own lives. They're running Loop 3 without Loop 1. The order is wrong. No amount of transcendence compensates for a broken foundation.

Ambition corrodes when growth replaces identity.

This is the achiever's trap. The insight here is about success, performance, capability. The belief is that if you accomplish enough, become competent enough, earn enough — then you'll feel solid.

But Loop 2 doesn't stabilize identity. It builds capacity. These are different things.

Here's what happens:

You achieve. You hit the target. For a moment, you feel good. Then the feeling fades. So you set a higher target. Achieve again. Feel good again. Watch it fade again.

The cycle accelerates. The targets get bigger. The feeling of satisfaction gets shorter. You're running faster on a wheel that isn't going anywhere.

The loop is running, but it's not addressing the actual problem. The actual problem is Loop 1 — you don't trust yourself at a foundational level. You're using achievement as a substitute for self-trust. Every win is a temporary patch over a permanent crack.

This explains the executive who builds a company and feels empty. The athlete who wins championships and feels nothing. The professional who climbs to the top and looks down at a view that means nothing to them.

They did everything right. They worked hard. They won. And none of it touched the actual problem.

This is why successful people feel hollow. Why high performers burn out. Why the person who has everything still feels like they're not enough.

They mastered the wrong loop. They built the capacity without stabilizing the foundation. The scaffolding is impressive. The building inside is empty.

Achievement without foundation is scaffolding. Looks impressive. Holds nothing.

The knowing-doing gap is not a motivation problem.

Everyone calls it motivation. "I know what to do, I can't get motivated." "I understand it, I need to find the willpower." "If I could get myself to do it."

This framing is wrong. And believing it keeps you stuck.

The gap between knowing and doing isn't filled with motivation. It's filled with trust. Specifically, self-trust. Loop 1.

Here's what's happening:

When the self-trust loop is intact, motivation isn't required. You say you'll do something, and you do it. Not because you feel motivated. Not because you summoned willpower. Because your system believes your word. The action follows because actions follow from a stable identity.

When the self-trust loop is broken, motivation becomes a constant struggle. You say you'll do something, and then you negotiate. You bargain. You wait to feel like it. You don't feel like it. You don't do it. The gap widens.

This isn't lack of motivation. This is lack of credibility. Your own system doesn't believe you'll follow through, so it won't fund the intention. Why would it? You've proven, through repeated non-action, that your promises don't mean anything.

More motivation won't fix this. More insight won't fix this. More understanding of why you're stuck won't fix this.

Only one thing fixes it: rebuilding the trust through action. Small, kept promises. Visible evidence. Loop repair.

The insight trap has three doors.

Door one: understanding becomes a substitute for action. You learn about the pattern. You explain the pattern. You feel like you're making progress because you understand more. But understanding is not change. The loop never gets engaged.

Door two: insight becomes a form of self-judgment. You understand your dysfunction, and now you hate yourself more precisely. You know exactly what's wrong with you. The insight doesn't liberate — it condemns. And the shame makes action even harder.

Door three: insight becomes a performance. You explain your patterns to others. You demonstrate self-awareness. You gain social credit for knowing yourself. But the performance replaces the repair. You become someone who talks about change than someone who changes.

All three doors lead to the same place: stuckness with better vocabulary.

The person behind door one can explain their procrastination in detail. They still procrastinate.

The person behind door two hates themselves with surgical precision. The hatred doesn't help.

The person behind door three is known for their self-awareness. Their life remains unchanged.

Insight without loop engagement is a room with no exit.

. . .

Real change requires a different approach.

Not more insight. Not deeper understanding. Not better explanations for why you are the way you are. Not another book, another podcast, another framework that explains your patterns more elegantly.

Real change requires loop engagement.

This means: identifying which loop is broken. Then running the correct repair sequence for that loop. Through action. Through evidence. Through the slow accumulation of trust that only comes from doing what you said you would do.

Chapter 1 introduced the loops. This chapter explains why knowing about them isn't enough.

The rest of this book is about engaging them.

Not through understanding. Through structure.

Not through insight. Through action.

The loops don't care what you know. They only care what you do.

Here's the hard truth.

You could put this book down right now. You could explain the three loops to a friend. You could pass a test on the material. You could discuss it intelligently at dinner.

And none of that would change anything.

Because the loops aren't updated by reading. They're not updated by understanding. They're not updated by knowing the theory.

They're updated by action. By kept promises. By evidence that accumulates. By the slow repair of a system that learned, through experience, what to believe.

Insight is where change starts to seem possible.

Action is where change happens.

The gap between those two things is where most people live their entire lives.

PART TWO
THE THREE LOOPS

The Three Loops, 2026 Ink, charcoal, acrylic, and gold on canvas 150 × 150 cm (59 × 59 in) Lee Powell (Keny)

CHAPTER 3
LOOP ONE: SELF-TRUST

Sedimentary accumulation. The darker foundation holds, while upper layers show weathering and trace marks—evidence of what was built, what remained, what eroded. Trust accretes slowly through repeated action. Each kept promise adds a layer. Each broken one leaves a mark.
Medium: Acrylic, charcoal, pigments and ink on canvas
Dimensions: 150 × 150 cm by Lee Powell, 2026

"Every broken promise is a vote against yourself. Enough votes and you stop running for office."

This is the foundation.

Everything else — growth, meaning, purpose, contribution — sits on top of this loop. When it's working, the rest of your life has something to stand on. When it's broken, everything built above it becomes unstable. Cosmetic. A performance without a performer.

The Self-Trust Loop governs one thing: whether you believe your own word.

Not whether others believe you. Whether *you* do.

Here's how it works.

Action → Evidence → Identity → Action

You take an action. Reality produces evidence. Your nervous system updates your identity based on that evidence. Your updated identity shapes the next action you take.

This cycle runs constantly. It's been running since you were a child. Every time you said you'd do something and did it, the loop registered. Every time you said you'd do something and didn't, the loop registered that too.

The loop doesn't evaluate intentions. It doesn't weigh circumstances. It doesn't care about your reasons, your mood, or how hard the day was.

It only tracks one thing: Did you do what you said you would do?

Yes builds trust. No erodes it. The math is simple. The consequences are not. Your body doesn't track what you meant. It tracks what you did.

This loop operates below language.

You can tell yourself anything. You can explain, justify, rationalize. You can construct elaborate narratives about why this time was different, why that failure doesn't count, why tomorrow will be the real start.

The loop doesn't hear any of it.

It registers behavior. That's all. The verbal, conscious part of your mind can spin whatever story it wants. The part that governs action isn't listening. It's watching. And it only updates based on what it sees.

This is why affirmations don't work for most people. You can stand in front of a mirror and tell yourself you're disciplined, confident, reliable. The loop knows better. It has the receipts. Every broken promise is on file.

You can't talk yourself into self-trust. You can only act yourself into it.

When this loop is working, certain things become easy.

You say you'll wake up early, and you wake up early. Not because you feel motivated. Because that's what you do. The identity is stable. The action follows.

You commit to a project, and you work on it. Not because someone's watching. Because you said you would. Your word means something—to you.

You set a boundary, and you hold it. Boundaries are what you keep, not what you announce.

You feel tired, but you do the thing anyway. Not from self-punishment. From alignment. The commitment holds. The feeling is irrelevant.

People with intact self-trust don't experience discipline as effort. They experience it as alignment. The action matches the intention. The system is coherent. There's no internal negotiation because there's nothing to negotiate.

This isn't willpower. It's architecture.

When this loop breaks, everything becomes harder.

The alarm goes off. Immediately, the negotiation starts. Five more minutes. I didn't sleep well. I'll start tomorrow. Today doesn't count.

You commit to something. Before you even begin, part of you is already calculating how to get out of it. The system doesn't believe you'll follow through. So it doesn't invest in the intention.

You make a plan. The plan feels good. Making the plan feels like progress. Then execution comes, and the plan evaporates. You're not sure how. It ... didn't happen.

This is what broken self-trust looks like from the inside. Chronic low-grade resistance. Everything feels heavy. Motivation comes in bursts and then disappears. You know what to do —you've always known—but knowing and doing feel like different countries, and you've lost your passport.

Motivation isn't a resource. It's a signal. When it's absent, the system has stopped believing you.

The failure signatures are consistent.

Endless planning without execution. The plan becomes the product. You refine systems, organize tools, research options. The planning itself provides the feeling of progress. Actual execution never arrives because planning is safer. Planning can't fail.

The gap between knowing and doing isn't motivation. It's trust. And you're the one who broke it.

The "I know what I should do" syndrome. You have the insight. You understand the pattern. You could explain your dysfunction to a therapist better than they could explain it to you. But nothing changes. Because knowing isn't the problem. Doing is. And the loop that governs doing is broken.

The gap between knowing and doing isn't motivation. It's trust. And you're the one who broke it.

Promises that dissolve. You commit with genuine intention. Monday will be different. This time you mean it. Then Monday comes, and somehow the commitment has lost its weight. It felt real when you made it. Now it feels optional. Negotiable. The promise made was not the promise kept.

Internal bargaining. Constant negotiation with yourself. If I skip today, I'll do double tomorrow. If I do this one thing, I can skip that other thing. The bargaining feels like strategy. It's erosion. Each negotiation teaches the system that your commitments are opening offers, not final terms.

Exhaustion without progress. You're tired, but you haven't done anything. The fatigue isn't from effort—it's from resistance. Fighting yourself takes energy. The gap between intention and action is metabolically expensive.

Insight without execution is a hobby. An expensive one.

This manifests differently depending on where you live your life.

In achievement contexts, it looks like serial starting. New projects, new systems, new Monday routines. The gym membership that becomes a monument to good intentions. The language app with a three-day streak and a six-month gap. Courses purchased, never completed. The excitement of beginning. The absence of following through.

In relational contexts, it looks like over-promising and under-delivering. Saying yes when you mean no. Agreeing to things and then resenting them. Committing to show up and then finding reasons not to. People learn not to count on you, and eventually, you learn it too.

It also looks like chronic people-pleasing that erodes self-trust from the inside. You say yes to requests you don't have capacity for. You agree to help when you're already depleted. You override your own boundaries to avoid disappointing others. Each time you abandon what you know you need in favor of what someone else wants, the loop registers: your word to yourself doesn't count. The pattern looks generous from the outside. From the inside, it's self-betrayal accumulation. Your system learns that everyone else's needs matter except your own.

Saying yes when you mean no. Chronic over-promising followed by quiet withdrawal.

In internal contexts, it looks like self-abandonment. Knowing what you need — rest, boundaries, honesty — and negotiating yourself out of it. Treating your own needs as suggestions than requirements. The quiet understanding that even you won't show up for yourself.

There's a physical signature too.
Broken self-trust doesn't live in your head. It lives in your body.
There's a particular kind of restlessness. Unable to settle. Always scanning for the next thing, the next distraction, the next escape from the discomfort of being with yourself. The body doesn't want to be still because stillness means feeling the gap between who you say you are and who you've been acting like.
There's a heaviness before action. The alarm goes off, and the body feels weighted. Not tired exactly — resistant. The system is bracing against an intention it doesn't believe will be honored.
There's a tightness in the chest when you make commitments. The words come out, but something constricts. The body knows the pattern. It's been here before. It's preparing for disappointment.
There's a specific flavor of shame. Not dramatic, not acute. Quiet. Persistent. The background hum of knowing you're not living according to your own word. It doesn't announce itself. It sits there, coloring everything slightly grey.
If you've felt these sensations, you've felt the physical residue of a broken self-trust loop.

I didn't lose self-trust in a dramatic moment.

THE THREE LOOPS THAT RUN YOUR LIFE

There was no scandal. No implosion. No single failure I could point to and say: that's where it broke.

It went quietly. The way erosion goes.

It started with small promises. I'll train tomorrow. I'll send that message tonight. I'll deal with this properly on Monday.

Each one felt harmless. Rational. I always had a reason. I was busy. I was tired. I had bigger things to handle. And I meant it—at least in the moment I said it.

That was the trap. I mistook good intentions for integrity.

Over time, something shifted. Not consciously. Somatically. Plans started to feel heavy before I even began. Motivation didn't disappear—it stopped responding. Discipline felt fake, like a performance I could still put on for others but no longer believed myself.

I'd sit down to plan my day and feel a quiet resistance in my body. As if some part of me was thinking: why should I believe you this time?

That was the moment I didn't want to look at.

The truth was simple and humiliating. My nervous system had learned from evidence. I had trained it not to trust my word.

I made a pact with my son once. For me, it was nicotine—thirty-five years of it, hiding behind lozenges no one could see. For him, something else. We shook hands. I broke it. The shame of that cut deeper than anything anyone else ever said to me.

Nothing dramatic had failed. But everything small had. And self-trust doesn't break from catastrophe. It erodes from repetition.

I didn't need insight. I'd had insight for years. I needed to stop lying to myself about what counted.

Here's what makes this loop particularly vicious. When it breaks, it breaks your capacity to repair it.

Repairing self-trust requires keeping promises to yourself. But if your system doesn't believe your promises, it won't invest in them. You're less likely to keep them. Trust erodes further. The next promise becomes even less believable.

The loop feeds itself in the wrong direction.

This is why people stay stuck for years. Decades. It's not lack of awareness. It's not lack of desire. It's not that they haven't tried hard enough. It's that the mechanism required for repair has been damaged. The tool you need to fix the machine is part of the machine that's broken.

The downward spiral is self-reinforcing. Each broken promise makes the next one harder to keep. Each failure adds evidence to the case against yourself. The system becomes increasingly certain that commitments are noise — sounds you make that don't predict behavior.

This is also why big, ambitious commitments usually make things worse. Your system already doesn't believe you. Now you're promising something huge. The gap between promise and probable outcome is so large that the system writes off the commitment immediately. You fail. Trust erodes further. The hole gets deeper.

The repair path isn't through grand gestures. It's through small, kept promises that rebuild credibility one brick at a time.

The repair principle is simple. Not easy — simple.

Promises must be small enough to keep.[1] One promise per day, completed within 24 hours, no stacking.

This is counterintuitive. When self-trust is broken, the instinct is to fix it with something big. A dramatic commitment. A complete overhaul. New year, new me.

That instinct is wrong. It's the same instinct that got you here.

Small promises work because they're believable. Your system might not believe you'll transform your life. But it might believe you'll drink a glass of water when you wake up. Make your bed. Send one email.

These seem trivial. They're not. Each kept promise — no

matter how small — is a data point. Evidence that your word means something. The loop registers it. Identity updates slightly. The next promise becomes slightly more believable.

This is how trust is rebuilt. Not through revelation. Through repetition.

Evidence must be visible.

The loop updates from evidence. If there's no evidence, there's no update.

This means the action needs to produce something you can see. A checked box. A completed task. A physical change in your environment. Something that proves, to the part of you that tracks these things, that the promise was kept.

Vague commitments produce vague evidence. "I'll be more productive" — how do you know when you've done it? "I'll work on my health" — what does that look like in practice?

Specific commitments produce clear evidence. "I'll write for fifteen minutes before checking my phone" — either you did or you didn't. "I'll walk around the block before noon" — verifiable.

The system needs proof. Give it proof. Your body doesn't track what you meant. It tracks what you did. Every broken promise is a vote against yourself.

Identity updates slowly.

This is the hardest part. You can keep a promise today, and tomorrow your system will still doubt you. One kept promise doesn't undo years of broken ones.

The repair is cumulative. Day after day of small, kept promises. Week after week of evidence accumulating. The identity doesn't shift all at once. It shifts in increments, grudgingly, as the weight of new evidence slowly outweighs the old.

This requires patience. Most people don't have it. They keep a few promises, don't feel different, conclude it's not working, and stop. The loop was starting to register the change. Now it registers another abandoned effort.

The people who rebuild self-trust aren't more disciplined. They're more patient. They understand that trust — with yourself or anyone else — isn't rebuilt in a moment. It's rebuilt through sustained consistency over time.

Here's what you cannot skip.

You cannot access purpose without self-trust. You can think about purpose. You can talk about it. But the pursuit of anything meaningful requires showing up, repeatedly, for something that doesn't pay off immediately. If your system doesn't believe you'll show up, you won't.

You cannot build sustainable growth without self-trust. You can push yourself in bursts. White-knuckle your way through a project. But sustainable growth requires consistent effort over time. If every commitment is a negotiation, you'll exhaust yourself before you build anything.

You cannot offer real contribution without self-trust. Service requires reliability. If you can't be relied upon by yourself, your contribution will be erratic, driven by guilt or mood than genuine capacity. That's not service. That's compensation.

Every other loop depends on this one.

This is why it comes first. Not because it's the most exciting. Because it's the most foundational.

Without it, nothing else holds.

The Self-Trust Loop is not about becoming a better person. It's about becoming a person whose word means something — starting with the person who hears it most: you.

That's the foundation everything else is built on.

CHAPTER 4
LOOP TWO: GROWTH / MASTERY

Structural ascent under tension. The forms climb but show strain—scaffolding that expands capacity while bearing its own weight. Growth is not frictionless. The marks record both the pushing and the cost. What's built must also be carried. Medium: Acrylic, charcoal, pigments and ink on canvas Dimensions: 150 × 150 cm by Lee Powell, 2026

"Achievement without foundation is scaffolding around an empty building."

This is the loop that builds things.

Skills. Careers. Capabilities. The ability to navigate complexity, solve problems, create value. Everything you can do that you couldn't do before — you built it here, in this loop.

The Growth Loop governs competence, strength, and expansion. It's where effort converts into capacity. Where challenge becomes capability. Where you become someone who can handle more than you could before.

This loop is necessary. It's also dangerous.

Because this is the loop that can consume you.

Here's how it works.

Discomfort → Skill → Capacity → Higher Standard → Discomfort

You enter deliberate discomfort. You do something difficult, something beyond your current ability. Something that strains what you can currently do. The difficulty produces adaptation. Your system responds to the demand by building what's needed to meet it. You acquire skill.

Skill increases capacity. You can do things you couldn't do before. Handle loads you couldn't handle. Navigate situations that would have overwhelmed you. Solve problems that would have stopped you.

As capacity increases, your standards rise. What used to feel like achievement now feels like baseline. What used to be hard is now normal. What used to require effort now happens automatically. The edge has moved.

So you seek the next edge. New discomfort. New challenge. New territory where you're not yet competent. The loop continues.

This is how humans become capable. This is how expertise develops, how careers advance, how strength accumulates. Every skill you have was forged in this cycle. Everything you can do now that you couldn't do before — it came through this loop.

This loop runs on effort.

Not intention. Not understanding. Not planning or dreaming or visualizing. Effort. Actual energy expended against actual resistance.

You can't think your way to competence. You can't wish yourself stronger. You can't read about skill acquisition and expect the skill to appear. The loop only turns when you push against something that pushes back.

This is what separates growth from insight. Insight happens in the mind. Growth happens in the collision between you and difficulty. The difficulty is required. Without it, there's nothing to adapt to.

This is also what makes this loop expensive. Every turn costs something. Energy, time, discomfort, risk of failure. The loop doesn't give capacity for free. It trades — effort for capability, discomfort for strength.

When this loop is working, certain things happen.

You get better. Not abstractly, not theoretically — measurably. Skills sharpen. Problems that used to stump you become solvable. Loads that used to crush you become manageable. There's evidence. Real evidence of increased capability.

Your range expands. More options, more capabilities, more ways to respond to what life throws at you. Competence creates freedom. The person who can do more things has more choices. The person with more skills has more moves.

Confidence follows — not the affirmation kind, but the

earned kind. You've been tested. You've survived. You know, from evidence, what you can handle. That knowledge changes how you move through the world.

There's a particular satisfaction in this loop that doesn't exist elsewhere. The satisfaction of having built something — even if that something is yourself. The satisfaction of difficulty overcome, of capacity earned, of being more capable than you were yesterday.

This satisfaction is real. It's also a trap.

The first failure mode is over-identification.

This is when the loop stops serving you and starts consuming you.

The pattern looks like this: You grow. You achieve. The achievement feels good. So you grow more. Achieve more. The feeling of growth becomes addictive. Somewhere along the way, your identity fuses with your output. You are what you produce. Your worth equals your performance.

Now the loop owns you.

Rest feels like failure. A day without measurable progress feels like a day wasted. Relationships become secondary — they don't produce output, so they don't count. Your body becomes a tool, a resource to be optimized and extracted from until it breaks down.

The standards keep rising. The bar that felt like achievement becomes the new minimum. You reach it, and immediately it moves higher. There's no arrival point. There's only more.

This is the achiever's trap. It looks like success from the outside. From the inside, it's a prison with nice windows.

Growth serves identity. When it replaces identity, you're building that prison yourself.

Over-identification has specific signatures.

The inability to stop. Not because there's more to do—

there's always more to do—but because stopping feels existentially threatening. If you're not producing, who are you?

Anxiety without crisis. Even when things are objectively fine, there's a low-grade hum of inadequacy. You should be doing more. You could be doing better. The present accomplishment is already insufficient.

Relational erosion. People become obstacles or instruments. The relationships that can't be justified by output quietly atrophy. You don't notice until you need someone and no one's there.

In relational contexts, over-identification looks different but follows the same pattern. You become the person everyone depends on. The organizer. The problem-solver. The one who holds everything together. Your competence expands into other people's lives—managing their emotions, solving their problems, carrying responsibilities that aren't yours. The growth is real. You're getting better at caregiving, at anticipating needs, at keeping systems running. But the loop is consuming you. Your identity fuses with being needed. Rest feels like abandoning people. Boundaries feel like failure. You're growing capacity in relational management while your own life remains unmanaged.

Physical breakdown. Sleep becomes negotiable. Exercise becomes another optimization target. The body sends signals — fatigue, pain, illness — and you override them. Until you can't.

The moving goalpost. Every achievement is immediately discounted. You got the promotion — but someone else got it faster. You hit the target — but the target was too easy. The win doesn't land. It reveals the next benchmark you're behind on.

People in this mode are successful by most external measures. They're also hollowing themselves out. The growth continues, but there's less and less person underneath to benefit from it.

When self-trust started slipping, I didn't slow down.

I sped up.

If I'm honest, growth became my workaround. My excuse for not looking closer. As long as I was building, shipping, achieving—something had to be okay. Right?

I told myself this was discipline. Ambition. High standards.

What it really was: distraction dressed up as purpose.

Growth gave me an identity I could still wear in public. Builder. Operator. The capable one. People trusted me because I was effective. I trusted myself because I was moving.

At least, I thought I did.

The problem with using growth as identity is that it never lets you stop. Rest feels like regression. Stillness feels like decay. You don't downshift—you brace harder.

I remember hitting milestones that should have felt satisfying. Deals closed. Products shipped. Recognition landed.

And the feeling I had wasn't pride.

It was relief.

Relief that I could keep going. Relief that I didn't have to stop and look too closely.

That's when I knew something was wrong.

Success didn't soften anything. It tightened the loop. My nervous system was always on. Always scanning. Always braced for the next demand.

I wasn't growing.

I was outrunning the quiet discomfort I didn't want to name.

Growth had become a substitute for self-trust. And substitutes always come due.

The second failure mode is avoidance.

This is when the loop is abandoned than overworked.

The pattern looks like this: Growth requires discomfort. Discomfort is unpleasant. So you avoid the discomfort. You tell yourself a story about why the growth isn't necessary. You're above it. You don't need to prove anything. You've opted out of the rat race.

But you haven't opted out. You've stopped growing.

Avoidance wears sophisticated disguises. It presents as wisdom, as enlightenment, as having transcended the petty concerns of achievement. "I don't need external validation." "I'm focused on being, not doing." "Success isn't everything."

These statements might be true. They might also be cover for stagnation.

The difference is felt, not stated. Someone who has genuinely transcended the growth loop has grown enough to know what they're transcending. They have capacity. They've built things. They've been tested and have the competence to show for it.

Someone who's avoiding the growth loop hasn't transcended it. They've bypassed it. They have the philosophy of someone who's been through the fire, without having been through the fire. It's wisdom without the receipts.

Avoidance has its own signatures.

Comfort disguised as peace. Everything is easy because nothing is attempted. The absence of struggle gets relabeled as contentment. But it's not contentment — it's stagnation dressed up in spiritual language.

Resentment toward those who grow. If you've truly opted out, other people's achievements wouldn't bother you. When they do — when you feel a flicker of envy or judgment toward someone who's pushing and winning — that's a signal. The loop isn't transcended. It's suppressed.

Capacity atrophy. Skills unused decay. Options unconsidered close. The range of what you can do shrinks over time. You may not notice it shrinking, but it's shrinking.

Identity inflation without foundation. The self-concept is grand. The capabilities don't match. There's a gap between who you think you are and what you can do. This gap produces a particular kind of fragility — the fragility of an identity that can't survive contact with a real test.

The un-lived life. Somewhere underneath the philosophy of opting out is the quiet knowledge that you didn't try. Didn't build what you could have built. Didn't become what you could have become. This produces its own kind of shame — not the shame of failure, but the shame of never having been in the arena.

This loop manifests differently depending on context.

In achievement contexts, over-identification looks like workaholism, burnout, and the endless chase of metrics that stopped meaning anything long ago. Burnout isn't too much work. It's the wrong loop for too long. Avoidance looks like chronic underperformance, jobs that are easy but unfulfilling, potential that never converts to reality.

In relational contexts, over-identification looks like becoming whoever others need you to be. Building social competence at the expense of private stability. Being excellent at managing everyone's life except your own. Avoidance looks like isolation justified as introversion, relationships that never deepen because depth requires the discomfort of vulnerability.

In internal contexts, over-identification looks like constant self-improvement with no arrival point. Reading books about life instead of living one. Another course, another framework, another system—while the actual life remains unexamined. Optimizing yourself like a machine without ever asking what the machine is for. Avoidance looks like fixed beliefs about your own limitations, comfort zones that never expand, a self-concept frozen in place.

The loop has a physical signature too.

Over-identification feels like tension that never releases. Shoulders at your ears. Jaw clenched. Sleep that doesn't restore. A body perpetually braced, never settling into genuine rest.

Avoidance feels different—heaviness without cause. Fatigue that isn't earned. A body that recoils from challenge not because the challenge is too hard but because any challenge feels like too much.

Both states are uncomfortable. Neither is sustainable.

Here's the regulation principle.

Growth must serve identity. It must never replace it.

This means the loop has to be bounded. There has to be a reason you're growing — something the growth is for beyond growth itself. Values that constrain the expansion. Limits that protect what matters. An identity solid enough to use capacity than being consumed by the chase for more of it.

Growth without boundaries is cancer. It expands until it kills the host.

The question isn't whether to engage this loop. You have to engage it. Competence matters. Capability matters. The ability to handle challenge matters. A life without growth is a life that slowly shrinks.

The question is whether you're running the loop or whether the loop is running you.

Are you growing toward something? Or just growing?

Is the expansion serving values you've chosen? Or has expansion become the only value?

Do you know when to stop? Or does the goalpost keep moving forever, keeping you in permanent deficit?

These questions don't answer themselves. The loop won't regulate itself.

There's also a dependency to remember.

Loop 2 doesn't function well without Loop 1.

Growth without self-trust produces achievement without stability. You build the career, but you're standing on a cracked foundation. You accumulate the wins, but they don't land because there's no solid self to receive them.

This is the achiever who feels hollow. Keeps winning. Keeps feeling like a fraud. Grows capacity without growing the person underneath.

If Loop 1 is broken, fix Loop 1 first. Growth will still be there. It will still be necessary. But it will work differently — landing, accumulating — once the foundation is solid.

Growth is not evil.

The cultural conversation sometimes treats ambition as a disease. Striving as a pathology. The desire to improve as something to be cured.

This is wrong. Competence matters. The ability to do difficult things matters. Expanding your capacity to handle what life throws at you — that matters.

The problem isn't growth. The problem is growth unbound. Growth that replaces identity instead of serving it. Growth for its own sake, disconnected from values, disconnected from meaning.

The loop itself is neutral. What you do with it isn't.

When it's regulated — bounded by values, grounded in self-trust, directed toward something that matters — this loop is how you build a capable life. It's how you become someone who can do something in the world.

That's worth doing.

The work is making sure that's all it does. Growth serves you. Not the other way around.

CHAPTER 5
LOOP THREE: MEANING / CONTRIBUTION

Dispersed impact, multiple nodes. Not a single center but a pattern of connection—effort distributed outward, touching what lies beyond the self. Meaning doesn't consolidate. It radiates. The structure is relational, not contained. Medium: Acrylic, charcoal, pigments and ink on canvas Dimensions: 150 × 150 cm by Lee Powell, 2026

"You don't find meaning. You become someone capable of carrying it."

This is the loop that answers the question the other loops can't.

Loop 1 asks: Can I trust myself?
Loop 2 asks: Can I become capable?
Loop 3 asks: Why bother?

You can trust yourself completely and still feel empty. You can be extraordinarily capable and still feel like none of it matters. Self-trust and competence are necessary — but they don't answer the question of what any of it is for.

That's what this loop does. It converts effort into meaning. It turns capability into contribution. It answers the question that survival, success, and self-improvement never touch: Why sustain the effort once you no longer have to?

Here's how it works.

Service → Impact → Significance → Responsibility → Service

You contribute something beyond yourself. Not for applause, not for reward — for the contribution itself. Your effort touches something outside your own skin.

Impact is felt. Someone or something is affected by what you did. The contribution lands. It matters to someone other than you.

Significance emerges internally. Not as a thought — as a felt sense. The effort meant something. There was a point to it. The work connected to something larger than the immediate task.

Responsibility expands. Because the contribution mattered, you're now accountable for more. The impact created obligations. People depend on what you built. The thing you served now requires continued service.

So you serve again. Deeper this time. More capable now. The loop continues.

This is how meaning accumulates. Not through discovery — through action. Not through finding your purpose — through becoming someone who can carry one.

This loop is different from the others.

Loop 1 is internal. It happens between you and yourself. Loop 2 is developmental. It happens between you and challenge. Loop 3 is relational. It happens between you and others. Between you and something larger than yourself.

Meaning isn't manufactured in isolation. It emerges in connection. In contribution. In the felt experience of mattering to something beyond your own comfort and survival.

This is why solitary achievement feels hollow. Why success without contribution rings empty. Why you can win every game and still feel like you're losing. The growth loop was running, but the meaning loop was starved.

Humans aren't built to only serve themselves. The system requires something to carry beyond the self. Without it, even the most successful life starts to taste like nothing.

When this loop is working, certain things happen.

Effort feels worthwhile even when it's hard. Not because it's fun, not because you're motivated — because it connects to something that matters. The difficulty is bearable because the contribution is real.

Hard days don't empty you completely. There's something underneath the fatigue that holds. A reason to get up tomorrow that isn't about personal gain. The tank isn't full, but it's not existentially empty either.

You know why you're doing what you're doing. Not in an abstract, philosophical sense — in a felt sense. The action connects to something beyond itself. The work has a direction that isn't "more."

There's a particular steadiness that comes from this loop. Not excitement, not motivation — steadiness. The person running a functioning meaning loop doesn't need to psych themselves up every morning. They know what they're serving. That knowledge is its own fuel.

The first failure mode is premature meaning.

This is when you try to run Loop 3 before Loops 1 and 2 are stable.

The pattern looks like this: You want to help. You want to matter. You want to contribute something significant. So you throw yourself into service — without having built the foundation first.

You try to save the world while your own life is falling apart. You give to others what you don't have for yourself. You offer stability you haven't earned, wisdom you haven't integrated, presence you can't sustain.

This isn't generosity. It's compensation. You're using Loop 3 to avoid the harder work of Loops 1 and 2.

The result is predictable: collapse. Boundary erosion. Martyrdom. You give until you're empty, then resent the people you gave to. You serve until you break, then blame the service. The contribution was real, but it was built on sand. When the foundation cracks, everything built on it falls.

Premature meaning has specific signatures.

Helping others while ignoring yourself. You're available for everyone else's crisis. Your own needs go unaddressed. The service feels urgent. Self-care feels selfish. This ratio is unsustainable. Somewhere you know it.

Boundaries that don't hold. You say yes when you mean no.

Overcommit, then either follow through at great cost or fail and feel guilty. The giving isn't clean—it comes with resentment attached.

Identity through service. You don't know who you are without someone to help. The contribution isn't an expression of a stable self—it's a substitute for one. Take away the helping, and there's no one underneath.

This pattern often begins in families where helping becomes survival. You learned early that your value came from managing other people's needs. Now it's the only identity you have. You help your partner manage emotions they should manage themselves. You solve problems for adult children who need to solve their own. You're the one friends call in crisis—but you have no one to call. The service is real. The depletion is real. But the foundation it's built on isn't stable—it's compensatory. You're using Loop 3 to avoid the Loop 1 work of learning to keep promises to yourself first.

Collapse cycles. Intense periods of giving followed by crashes. You pour yourself out, empty completely, withdraw to recover, then do it again. The pattern repeats because the underlying structure never changed.

Contempt for the helped. This is the dark signature. Somewhere underneath all the service, there's a quiet resentment. You're giving so much. Why aren't they grateful enough? Why don't they change? This contempt reveals the truth: the service was never clean. It was a transaction disguised as a gift.

People in this mode look generous. They look caring. They look like they've found their purpose. They're running from the foundation they never built.

The second failure mode is meaning starvation.

This is when Loops 1 and 2 are running, but Loop 3 is neglected.

The pattern looks like this: You've built the foundation. You trust yourself. You've developed competence, achieved things, accumulated capability. By external measures, you've won.

And it tastes like nothing.

There's no contribution. No service. No connection to anything beyond your own advancement.[1] The growth was real, but it went nowhere. The capability exists, but it isn't used for anything that matters.

This is the successful person who feels hollow. The achiever who wonders what the point is. The person who did everything right and still lies awake asking: Is this all there is?

Meaning starvation has its own signatures.

Success that doesn't satisfy. You hit the target. The feeling lasts a day, maybe a week. Then it's gone, and you're chasing the next target. The wins accumulate. The satisfaction doesn't.

The "what's the point" question. It starts quietly. A background hum during routine tasks. Then it gets louder. You find yourself unable to answer why you're doing what you're doing — and the inability bothers you.

Cynicism as sophistication. You've seen enough to know that nothing matters. Purpose is a fantasy. Meaning is a story people tell themselves. This position feels intelligent. It's a defense against disappointment — if nothing matters, you can't be hurt by caring.

Nihilism dressed as realism. Everything is pointless. Everyone is self-interested. Contribution is naive. Philosophical nihilism dressed as sophistication. Cynicism as protection against disappointment. The worldview is bleak, but it's presented as clear-eyed truth-telling. Underneath it is the unaddressed ache of a meaning loop that was never fed.

Midlife collapse. This is meaning starvation coming due. Decades of growth without contribution, achievement without purpose, success without significance. The bill arrives. The question that was always there becomes impossible to ignore: What was any of it for?

For a long time, I assumed meaning would arrive later.

After the next milestone. After the next win. After things settled down.

Meaning felt like something you earned—a reward at the end of enough effort.

So I postponed it.

Then I reached places I'd been aiming for. Not fantasy versions. Real ones. Oxford. Businesses built. Revenue generated. Products shipped. Recognition from people whose opinions I'd valued.

And nothing collapsed.

But nothing completed either.

There was no despair. No drama. Just a flat, confusing absence. A quiet sense that I was standing where I'd aimed to stand—and it wasn't answering the question I'd hoped it would.

That's a hard thing to admit. It sounds ungrateful. Like you're rejecting what others would give anything for.

But the truth is simpler: success doesn't install meaning. It only amplifies whatever you brought with you.

I hadn't brought any.

I'd chased coherence through achievement, only to find myself holding outcomes that didn't tell me who I was or why any of it mattered.

Meaning can't be deferred until after the act. If it isn't present before you begin, it won't magically appear when you arrive.

I learned that too late the first time.

That wasn't a failure of success. It was a failure of sequence.

This loop manifests differently depending on context.

In achievement contexts, premature meaning looks like building a charity while your business is failing. Launching a movement while your personal life implodes. Grand visions, no operational foundation. Meaning starvation looks like empires that feel like prisons. Winning without caring. Success that tastes like ash.

In relational contexts, premature meaning looks like being everyone's therapist while you're falling apart inside. Saving your partner instead of building with them. Parenting from depletion. Meaning starvation looks like isolation masked as independence. Relationships that never deepen into mutual care. Being known for what you've achieved, but not known at all.

In internal contexts, premature meaning looks like spiritual ambition without grounded practice. Seeking enlightenment while ignoring your body, your finances, your commitments. Meaning starvation looks like philosophical nihilism. The quiet conclusion that nothing matters, arrived at not through wisdom but through starvation. The un-lived life justified by sophisticated arguments.

The loop has a physical signature.

Premature meaning feels like depletion that won't resolve. Giving and giving without replenishment. A body that's chronically tired because it's being asked to run on empty. The exhaustion of pouring from an empty vessel.

Meaning starvation feels like hollowness behind the sternum. A particular emptiness that isn't hunger or fatigue — it's the absence of something to carry. A body that's well-maintained but purposeless. All the vitality with no direction for it to go.

Both states are depleting. One from over-giving, one from under-connecting. Neither is sustainable.

Rest isn't recovery if you're running from yourself. It's just a change of scenery for your exhaustion.

Here's the hard truth about this loop.

You don't find meaning. You become someone capable of

carrying it. Most people try to pick up the weight before they've built the back.

This is the fundamental error in most discussions of purpose. People treat meaning like a destination — something to be discovered, located, arrived at. As if meaning is out there somewhere, waiting to be found, and once you find it everything will make sense.

That's not how it works.

Meaning isn't found. It's built. Through contribution. Through service. Through the slow accumulation of impact that comes from showing up, repeatedly, for something beyond yourself.

But you can only build meaning if you're capable of sustaining the effort. And that requires Loops 1 and 2 to be functional first.

This is why "finding your purpose" before building your foundation is a trap. You might find something that looks like purpose. You might feel inspired, excited, aligned. But if the foundation isn't there, you can't carry what you found. The meaning collapses under the weight of your own instability.

The order matters.

There's a dependency structure here.

Loop 3 doesn't function without Loops 1 and 2.

Without Loop 1, you can't sustain contribution. Service requires showing up repeatedly. If you can't keep promises to yourself, you won't keep promises to what you serve.

Without Loop 2, you can't contribute effectively. Service requires capability. Good intentions without competence don't help anyone. The desire to contribute without the capacity to contribute is noise.

This is why the sequence matters. Build the foundation. Develop the capacity. Then — and only then — direct that capacity toward something that matters beyond yourself.

Meaning earned this way is stable. It doesn't collapse when things get hard. It doesn't deplete you. It draws from a full vessel, not an empty one.

Meaning is not opposed to achievement.

Some frameworks treat service as the opposite of ambition. As if you have to choose between building something for yourself and contributing to others.

This is a false choice. The question isn't whether to achieve or contribute. It's whether the achievement connects to something beyond itself.

Growth without meaning is empty. Meaning without growth is ineffective. The integration of both — capacity directed toward contribution — is where a life becomes both capable and worthwhile.

This loop isn't the end of ambition. It's the direction for it. The thing that makes the effort worth sustaining past the point of personal necessity.

The Meaning Loop is where effort becomes worthwhile.

Not through philosophy. Not through discovery. Through service. Through contribution. Through the lived experience of mattering to something beyond your own survival.

This loop can't be rushed. It can't be faked. It can't be run on an unstable foundation.

But when it's running—built on self-trust, fueled by real capacity, directed toward genuine contribution—it answers the question that nothing else can.

Why bother?

Because this matters. Because the effort connects to something that will outlast the effort itself.

That's meaning. Not found. Earned.

CHAPTER 6
HOW THE LOOPS INTERACT

"The loops either support each other or undermine each other. They don't stay neutral."

The loops don't run in isolation.
They interact. They depend on each other. They can support each other or undermine each other. What happens in one loop affects what's possible in the others.

Understanding each loop separately is necessary. Understanding how they work together is where the model becomes useful.

The first thing to understand: the loops are hierarchical but concurrent.

Hierarchical means there's an order. A dependency structure. Some loops require others to be functional before they can work properly.

Concurrent means they're all running at the same time. You don't finish one and then start the next. All three are always operating, always updating, always influencing your life.

This creates a particular challenge. You can't focus on one

loop while completely ignoring the others. But you also can't treat them as interchangeable. The hierarchy matters. The sequence matters.

Get the sequence wrong, and you build on a cracked foundation.

Here's the ordering rule.

Loop 1 must be intact before Loop 2 functions well.

Self-trust is the foundation. If you can't keep promises to yourself, you can't sustain the effort that growth requires. You might push in bursts. You might white-knuckle through projects. But consistent, sustainable growth — the kind that compounds over time — requires a system that believes its own commitments.

Growth without self-trust produces achievement without stability. You build things, but they don't feel like yours. You accumulate wins, but they don't land. The external evidence of success piles up while the internal experience remains hollow.

This is the high achiever who feels like a fraud. Who keeps winning and keeps waiting to feel like a winner. The growth is real. The foundation isn't. So nothing built on it feels solid.

Loop 2 must be bounded before Loop 3 functions well.

Meaning requires capacity. Service requires capability. You can't contribute effectively if you haven't developed the competence to help. Good intentions without skill don't serve anyone.

But more than that — Loop 3 requires Loop 2 to be regulated, not present. If growth has consumed your identity, you have nothing left to give. If achievement has become the only value, contribution will always be subordinated to performance.

Meaning without growth is ineffective. Growth without meaning is empty. The integration requires both — but it requires growth to be in service of something, not an end in itself.

Loop 3 must be earned, not assumed.

You don't get to skip to meaning. You don't get to bypass the foundation and the development and arrive directly at purpose. Meaning that isn't built on self-trust and capability is unstable. It collapses under pressure. It produces martyrs, not contributors.

The sequence isn't arbitrary. It reflects structural reality. Each loop provides something the next one needs.

When the sequence is violated, predictable things break.

Meaning before self-trust produces hypocrisy and collapse.

You try to serve others while you can't serve yourself. You offer stability you don't have. You make commitments you can't keep. The contribution is real, but it's coming from an empty vessel.

Eventually, the gap between what you're offering and what you possess becomes unsustainable. You burn out. You collapse. Or worse — you become someone who preaches what they can't practice, who helps others with problems they haven't solved in themselves.

This is the helper who falls apart. The leader who can't lead their own life. The giver who secretly resents everyone they give to.

Growth before self-trust produces burnout and fraudulence.

You build the career, hit the targets, accumulate the achievements — all while standing on a cracked foundation. The external structure looks impressive. The internal experience is exhaustion and imposter syndrome.

Every win feels temporary because there's no stable self to receive it. Every achievement immediately becomes the new minimum because achievement is being used to compensate for a missing foundation, not to express a solid one.

This is burnout. Not too much work — wrong sequence. The growth wasn't grounded. The effort wasn't building on anything stable. So it extracted and extracted until there was nothing left.

Growth without meaning produces emptiness.

Loop 2 running hard, Loop 3 starved. You get better and better at things that matter less and less. You climb ladders leaning against walls you never chose. You win games you don't care about.

The capability is real. The competence is genuine. But it's not connected to anything beyond itself. The growth goes nowhere. The effort has no direction except more.

This is the successful person asking "is this all there is?" The achiever who won everything and feels nothing. The professional at the top of their field, looking at a view that means nothing to them.

Meaning without growth produces sentimentality.

You care deeply but can't do anything about it. You want to help but lack the capability to contribute. The intention is beautiful. The impact is negligible.

This is the person with big visions and no operational capacity. Who wants to change the world but can't manage their own calendar. Who feels meaningful without producing meaning.

Caring isn't contribution. Intention isn't impact. Meaning without the growth to actualize it is sentiment — emotionally satisfying, practically useless.

Beyond sequence violations, there's another pattern to understand: compensation.

When one loop breaks, humans don't suffer the break. They compensate. They use another loop to fill the gap. This compensation feels like it's working — it provides temporary relief — but it makes the underlying problem harder to see and harder to fix.

Broken Loop 1, compensate with Loop 2.

Self-trust is damaged. You can't rely on yourself. Instead of repairing the foundation, you throw yourself into achievement. If you accomplish enough, maybe you'll finally feel solid.

You won't. The growth can't fix the foundation. But it can distract from the crack. Every new project, every new goal, every new mountain to climb keeps you from having to face the quiet truth: you don't trust your own word.

This is the achiever who can't stop. Who fills every moment with productivity. Who experiences rest as threat. The activity isn't growth — it's avoidance wearing achievement's clothes.

Broken Loop 1, compensate with Loop 3.

Self-trust is damaged. Instead of rebuilding it, you skip to service. Helping others feels better than facing yourself. Contribution provides identity when your own identity is fractured.

But the service isn't clean. It comes from depletion, not abundance. It's driven by need, not capacity. And it produces the martyrdom pattern — giving until empty, resenting those you gave to, collapsing, then starting again.

This is the helper who's running from themselves. Whose generosity is a hiding place. Who serves everyone except the person most in need of their attention: themselves.

Broken Loop 2, compensate with Loop 3.

Growth is avoided. Capability isn't developed. Instead of doing the hard work of becoming competent, you focus on meaning. You orient toward service, contribution, purpose — without building the capacity to deliver on any of it.

This feels elevated. It looks spiritual. It produces nothing but warm feelings and unrealized intentions. The meaning is genuine. The ability to actualize it isn't.

Broken Loop 3, compensate with Loop 2.

Meaning is starved. Instead of addressing the emptiness, you double down on growth. If you achieve more, build more, earn more — maybe the hollowness will fill.

It won't. More capacity doesn't create direction. More achievement doesn't generate purpose. But the activity can drown out the question. Keep moving fast enough, and you don't have to feel how empty the destination is.

This is the workaholic running from meaninglessness. The

achiever who's terrified of the question they've been avoiding. The successful person who can't slow down because slowing down means feeling what they've been outrunning.

These patterns explain most of the confusion you see — in yourself and in others.

The high achiever feeling hollow isn't broken. They've sequenced wrong. They built Loop 2 without stabilizing Loop 1, or they ran Loop 2 without feeding Loop 3. The achievement is real. The sequence isn't.

The spiritual person feeling ineffective isn't lacking commitment. They've skipped steps. They oriented toward Loop 3 without building the foundation or the capacity. The intention is beautiful. The structure is missing.

The helper who keeps burning out isn't too generous. They're compensating. They're using Loop 3 to avoid Loop 1. The service is real. The motivation isn't what it appears.

The driven person who can't stop isn't dedicated. They're trapped. Loop 2 has become a hiding place than a development path. The growth is real. The purpose is missing.

Once you see the pattern, you see it everywhere. In yourself. In the people around you. In the cultural scripts that keep promising solutions while delivering more of the same confusion.

The loops also interact in positive ways.

When the sequence is correct, each loop strengthens the others.

Stable Loop 1 makes Loop 2 sustainable.

When you trust yourself, growth isn't desperate. You can push without fear of collapse. You can rest without guilt.[1] The effort comes from solidity, not from trying to create solidity through effort.

Growth built on self-trust compounds. It accumulates. It lands. Each capability earned is integrated, not added to a pile of achievements that don't feel like yours.

Bounded Loop 2 makes Loop 3 effective.

When growth serves identity than replacing it, capacity becomes available for contribution. You have something to give — real capability, real skill, real competence — that can help.

And because the growth is bounded, you're not using achievement to avoid meaning. The capacity is available. The direction becomes the question, not the distraction.

Active Loop 3 gives Loop 2 direction.

When meaning is present, growth has somewhere to go. Development isn't random self-improvement — it's targeted capability building. You grow toward something. The effort has purpose.

This changes the experience of growth entirely. It's not about accumulating for accumulation's sake. It's about becoming capable of contributing what you're here to contribute.

Active Loop 3 reinforces Loop 1.

When you're serving something that matters, keeping promises to yourself becomes easier. The action connects to something beyond immediate gratification or discomfort avoidance. Self-trust isn't about trusting yourself — it's about trusting yourself to show up for what matters.

This creates a positive spiral. Meaning motivates follow-through. Follow-through builds self-trust. Self-trust enables sustainable growth. Sustainable growth increases capacity for contribution. Contribution deepens meaning.

The loops, when properly sequenced, become mutually reinforcing. Each one strengthens the others. The system becomes coherent.

This is what coherence looks like.

Not perfection. Not all loops running at maximum. Not some idealized state of permanent balance.

Coherence means: the right loop for the right problem. Self-trust when the foundation needs stabilizing. Growth when capability needs building. Meaning when direction needs clarifying.

Coherence means: proper sequence. Not skipping to Loop 3 to avoid Loop 1. Not running Loop 2 to compensate for Loop 3 starvation. Each loop built on what it requires, serving what comes next.

Coherence means: integration. The loops supporting each other than competing. Growth in service of meaning. Meaning built on stable ground. Self-trust enabling both.

That's the target. Not running all loops perfectly. Running them in the right order, for the right reasons, with the right boundaries.

The machinery exists. It's already running. The question is whether it's running coherently — or whether the loops are fighting each other, compensating for each other, undermining what they're supposed to support.

The next section of this book is about diagnosis: figuring out which loop is broken, which loop you're using to compensate, and what sequence of repair would help.

Because knowing the loops exist isn't enough. You have to know which one needs your attention right now.

PART THREE
DIAGNOSIS WITHOUT SHAME

CHAPTER 7
WHICH LOOP IS BROKEN?

"Most people are applying massive effort to the wrong loop."

You've seen the machinery. Three loops. How they work. How they fail. How they interact.

Now comes the harder question: Which one is broken in you?

This isn't abstract. The answer determines what you should do next. Get it wrong, and you'll apply effort to the wrong system — which is how people stay stuck for years while feeling like they're trying.

Get it right, and the path becomes clear. Not easy. Clear.

The first diagnostic is symptom-based.

Different loop failures produce different experiences. The feeling of broken self-trust is distinct from the feeling of meaning starvation. They might coexist, they might feed each other, but they're not the same thing.

Start by noticing what dominates your inner experience. Not what you think should be the problem — what is. The symptom that's most persistent, most present, most corrosive to your daily life.

Here's a mapping:

If your primary experience is...

Can't trust myself to follow through — Loop 1 is broken. The foundation is cracked. You know what to do, you intend to do it, and then you don't. The gap between knowing and doing is where you live.

Burnt out but still productive — Loop 2 is dysregulated. The growth loop is running too hard, extracting too much, bounded by nothing. You're producing output while hollowing yourself out.

Successful but empty — Loop 3 is starved. You've built capability, maybe even built an impressive life. But it's not connected to anything that matters. The achievement is real. The meaning isn't.

Spiritual but ineffective — Loop 2 has been bypassed. You have the philosophy of transcendence without the competence to actualize anything. The insight is real. The capability to do something with it isn't.

Driven but hollow — Loop 3 is starved while Loop 2 runs unchecked. All growth, no direction. The engine is powerful. It's not going anywhere that matters.

Insight-rich, action-poor — Loop 1 is broken. You understand everything. You change nothing. The knowing is sophisticated. The doing is absent.

Helping everyone, falling apart yourself — Loop 3 is running without Loop 1. Contribution without foundation. Service as avoidance. You're pouring from an empty vessel.

Can't stop, can't rest — Loop 2 has replaced identity. Achievement isn't serving you anymore. You're serving it. Rest feels like threat because stopping means feeling what you've been outrunning.

Everything feels pointless — Loop 3 is starved to the point of collapse. The cynicism isn't wisdom. It's the meaning loop shutting down. Nothing matters because nothing has been given a chance to matter.

Chronic exhaustion without accomplishment — Loop 1 is broken. The fatigue isn't from effort. It's from fighting yourself. The energy goes into resistance, negotiation, the metabolic cost of the gap between intention and action.

The second diagnostic is question-based.

Sometimes symptoms overlap. Sometimes you can't tell what's primary. These questions cut through the ambiguity.

For Loop 1 (Self-Trust):

When you make a commitment to yourself — yourself, no external accountability — how confident are you that you'll follow through?

If the honest answer is "not very," Loop 1 needs attention.

When the alarm goes off, does negotiation begin immediately? When you plan something, do you already suspect you won't do it? When you promise yourself rest, do you rest?

The self-trust loop is broken when your own word means nothing to you. When promises to yourself are treated as suggestions. When the system has stopped believing you'll show up.

For Loop 2 (Growth):

Can you rest without guilt? Can you have a day without measurable output and not feel like you're failing?

If rest feels like threat, if unproductive time triggers anxiety, Loop 2 has become dysregulated. Growth has stopped serving you and started consuming you.

Alternatively: Are you avoiding challenge? Have you built a life where nothing is difficult? Do you have sophisticated reasons for why you don't need to push yourself?

If comfort has become the goal, if you've philosophized your way out of growth, Loop 2 has been abandoned. The avoidance might look like wisdom. It's stagnation.

For Loop 3 (Meaning):

Does your effort connect to anything beyond yourself? Is there something you serve that isn't about your own advancement?

If the honest answer is no — if everything you do is ultimately about your own success, comfort, or status — Loop 3 is starved.

When you imagine your work or life stripped of external rewards, does anything remain that feels worthwhile? Or does it all become pointless without the recognition, the money, the achievement?

The meaning loop is starved when effort can't justify itself beyond personal gain. When "why bother" becomes a question you can't answer. When success doesn't satisfy because it was never connected to anything larger than the success itself.

The third diagnostic is about compensation.

This is crucial. Humans don't suffer broken loops — they compensate for them. They use one loop to avoid dealing with another. This compensation creates confusion because it looks like effort, like progress, like trying.

But it's effort in the wrong direction. Progress toward the wrong goal. Trying that makes the actual problem harder to fix.

The compensation patterns:

Using Loop 2 to avoid Loop 1:

You can't trust yourself, so you throw yourself into achievement. If you accomplish enough, maybe you'll finally feel solid. The activity is constant. The productivity is high. The foundation remains cracked.

This looks like dedication. It's avoidance. The growth isn't landing because there's no stable self to receive it. Every win evaporates because nothing underneath can hold it.

Signal: You're highly productive but feel like a fraud.

Achievements don't stick. You need the next goal immediately because stopping means feeling the emptiness.

Using Loop 3 to avoid Loop 1:

You can't trust yourself, so you orient toward service. Helping others feels better than facing your own broken promises. Contribution gives you identity when your own identity is fractured.

This looks like generosity. It's hiding. You serve everyone except yourself. The giving is real, but it's coming from depletion, not abundance. Eventually, you burn out or start resenting the people you help.

Signal: You're always available for others, never for yourself. Your own needs are perpetually deferred. You feel noble about this, but also exhausted and quietly resentful.

Using Loop 3 to avoid Loop 2:

You don't want to do the hard work of becoming competent, so you skip to meaning. You orient toward purpose, contribution, changing the world — without building the capacity to do any of it.

This looks spiritual. It's bypassing. The intention is beautiful. The capability to execute it is absent. You feel meaningful without producing meaning.

Signal: Big visions, no operational capacity. You care deeply but can't seem to translate caring into impact. Your sense of purpose exceeds your ability to actualize it.

Using Loop 2 to avoid Loop 3:

Meaning is starved, so you double down on growth. If you achieve more, build more, optimize more — maybe the hollowness will fill. The activity drowns out the question you're avoiding.

This looks driven. It's running. You can't slow down because slowing down means feeling how empty the destination is. The achievement is real. The purpose is missing.

Signal: You can't stop. Rest feels dangerous. You're successful by external measures but can't answer why any of it matters. The question "is this all there is?" haunts you.

The fourth diagnostic: What are you afraid of?

Sometimes the broken loop is the one you're most reluctant to look at.

If the idea of making tiny, daily promises to yourself feels pointless or beneath you — Loop 1 needs attention. The resistance is diagnostic.

If the idea of pushing into discomfort, building capability, competing or achieving feels threatening or distasteful — Loop 2 needs attention. The avoidance is diagnostic.

If the idea of serving something beyond yourself, contributing without recognition, mattering to others feels naive or scary — Loop 3 needs attention. The cynicism is diagnostic.

The loop you dismiss most quickly is often the loop most in need of repair.

A note on multiple breaks.

The loops can break simultaneously. You can have a cracked foundation and a starved meaning loop at the same time. You can have dysregulated growth and broken self-trust running together.

This is common. The loops influence each other, and a break in one often stresses the others. Years of compensating for broken self-trust with frantic achievement can simultaneously dysregulate Loop 2 and starve Loop 3. The patterns compound.

But repairs still have to be sequenced.

If multiple loops are broken, start with Loop 1. Always. The foundation has to be stabilized before anything else works properly. You can't regulate growth if you can't keep promises to yourself. You can't build meaning if you can't show up consistently.

Loop 1 first. Then Loop 2. Then Loop 3.

This might feel frustrating. You might want to skip to meaning, to purpose, to contribution. The foundation work feels unglamorous. Small promises feel trivial compared to big visions.

That frustration is itself a signal. The desire to skip the foundation is often the pattern that broke the foundation in the first place. The same impatience that led you to abandon Loop 1 for something more exciting is now telling you the repair is beneath you.

It isn't. The sequence isn't arbitrary. It's architectural.

You can't build the second floor while the first floor is cracked. And the cracks don't disappear because you've decided to focus on the roof.

Start where the structure requires. Not where your ambition wants to start. Not where the work feels most meaningful. Where the foundation needs repair.

The point of diagnosis isn't to label yourself.

It's not about identifying what's wrong with you. It's about identifying where intervention would help.

Most people are applying effort to the wrong loop. They're trying to find meaning when they need to rebuild self-trust. They're pushing for growth when they need to regulate the growth they already have. They're optimizing endlessly when they need to connect their capacity to something worth serving.

The effort isn't the problem. The direction is.

This is why people can try hard for years and stay stuck. The trying was real. The location was wrong. All that energy, pointed at the wrong system. All that work, unable to produce the change it was aimed at because it was aimed at the wrong target.

Diagnosis tells you where to point. Not what you are — what needs attention. Not who you're failing to be — which system needs repair.

That's the shift. From "what's wrong with me" to "which loop needs work."

The first question produces shame. The second produces action.

And action, directed at the right loop, is what changes things.

Once you know which loop is broken, the next question is how to repair it.

That's what the following chapters address — specific protocols for each loop, designed to rebuild what's been damaged and regulate what's been running unchecked.

But the protocols only work if you're applying them to the right loop.

Diagnosis first. Then repair.

You can't fix the machine if you don't know which part is broken.

CHAPTER 8
RELATIONAL LOOPS

"Loop states spread between people. What you're compensating for, they're learning to navigate."

The loops don't run in isolation. Neither do you.

Everything discussed so far has focused on your loops — how they work, how they break, how they interact within you. But humans don't exist alone. You live in relationships. And relationships create a second layer of loop dynamics that can either support your repair or undermine it completely.

Your loops interact with other people's loops. Sometimes that interaction is stabilizing. Often it isn't.

Here's the basic principle.

Other people's loop patterns affect yours. Your loop patterns affect theirs. These effects happen whether anyone is aware of them or not.

A partner with a broken self-trust loop creates instability you have to navigate. A friend stuck in growth-as-identity puts pressure on your own relationship with achievement. A parent who ran meaning without foundation models a pattern you may have inherited without choosing it.

You didn't select these influences. But you're living with them.

This doesn't mean other people are to blame for your broken loops. Your loops are yours to repair. But it does mean that understanding the relational dimension helps you see why repair can be harder than it looks on paper — and what to do about it.

I learned this the hard way.

When I'm overwhelmed—when too many demands converge and my nervous system starts redlining—I withdraw. Not dramatically. I go quiet. I need time to process, to integrate, to find my footing before I can respond clearly.

For years, I believed this was responsible. I was protecting the relationship from my unprocessed state. I was being thoughtful. I was avoiding saying something I'd regret.

What I didn't understand: silence without context isn't neutral.

To me, withdrawal felt like care. To the person waiting on the other side of my silence, it felt like abandonment. Like punishment. Like being locked out without knowing what they'd done wrong.

I told myself: if I don't say anything, I won't make it worse.

The truth: I was making it worse by saying nothing.

The damage wasn't from what I said in those moments. It was from the ambiguity I created by disappearing. My processing time became their anxiety. My regulation strategy became their destabilization.

I wasn't wrong to need space. I was wrong to take it without narration.

The fix wasn't becoming someone who doesn't need to withdraw. The fix was learning to say: "I'm overwhelmed. I need some time to process. This isn't about you. I'll be back."

Twenty words. That's all it took to change the impact of a pattern I'd been running for decades.

Silence without context is impact without intention. You might be regulating yourself. The other person is experiencing abandonment. Both things can be true at once.

Your loops don't run in isolation. Neither does your repair. The people closest to you are affected by patterns you might not even see as patterns.

The first pattern: loop contagion.

Loop states spread between people in close contact.

If you live with someone whose Loop 1 is broken — someone who chronically doesn't follow through, who negotiates every commitment, whose word means nothing — that pattern creates pressure on your own self-trust. You start adapting to their unreliability. You lower your expectations. You may even begin mirroring the pattern, because the environment normalizes it.

If you work with someone whose Loop 2 is dysregulated — someone who can't stop, who treats rest as failure, who measures everything by output — that pattern creates pressure on your own relationship with growth. You start feeling inadequate by comparison. You may push harder than you need to, not because it serves you, but because the environment demands it.

If you're close to someone whose Loop 3 is starved — someone cynical, someone who's concluded that nothing matters, someone who mocks meaning and contribution — that pattern creates pressure on your own sense of purpose. You start doubting whether your efforts toward meaning are naive. The cynicism seeps in.

Loop contagion isn't about weak boundaries. It's about proximity. The people you spend the most time with shape what feels normal. And what feels normal shapes what you do.

· · ·

The second pattern: complementary dysfunction.

Sometimes two people's broken loops lock together in a way that feels stable but isn't.

The classic version: one person with broken Loop 1 pairs with someone running Loop 3 as compensation. The first person can't trust themselves. The second person builds identity through helping. They find each other. It feels like a match.

The helper gets someone to help. The helped gets someone to lean on. Both needs are met. Neither loop gets repaired.

In fact, the arrangement prevents repair. The helper needs someone broken to help — so they unconsciously resist their partner's growth. The helped needs someone to compensate for their missing foundation — so they never build one.

This is codependency described in loop terms. Two compensatory patterns that interlock. Two people who need each other's dysfunction to maintain their own.

It can look like love. It can feel like connection. It's two people using each other to avoid the work they need to do alone.

Complementary dysfunction has many configurations.

The achiever and the supporter. One person runs Loop 2 compulsively. The other organizes their life around supporting that achievement — managing the household, the emotions, the logistics. The achiever gets to keep achieving without addressing what they're running from. The supporter gets identity through service without ever developing their own capacity. Both loops stay broken.

The meaning-seeker and the cynic. One person is oriented toward Loop 3, seeking purpose, trying to contribute. The other has starved Loop 3 and adopted cynicism as protection. They argue constantly about whether anything matters. But neither changes — the meaning-seeker gets to feel superior, the cynic gets to feel realistic. The conflict itself becomes the relationship's structure.

The collapsed and the rescuer. One person's loops are badly broken — maybe all three. The other swoops in to fix them, running premature Loop 3 without stable Loops 1 or 2. The collapsed person never has to repair because someone else is always managing. The rescuer never has to face their own foundation because they're too busy with someone else's.

In all these patterns, the relationship stabilizes around mutual dysfunction. It feels necessary. It feels like intimacy. It's a system designed to prevent growth.

The third pattern: loop pressure from family systems.

You didn't choose your first loop models. You inherited them.

Parents running dysregulated Loop 2 teach children that worth equals output. The child grows up believing rest is weakness, that achievement is the only valid source of identity. The loop pattern transfers across generations.

Parents with broken Loop 1 teach children that commitments are negotiable. The child grows up watching promises dissolve, learning that words and actions don't have to match. They inherit the crack in the foundation.

Parents running premature Loop 3 — helping everyone, falling apart themselves — teach children that service means self-abandonment. The child grows up believing that caring for yourself is selfish, that boundaries are unkind. They inherit martyrdom as a model of meaning.

These patterns aren't destiny. But they are starting points. The loop configurations you saw modeled in childhood become your defaults until you consciously build something different.

The fourth pattern: relationships that enable avoidance.

Some relationships make it easier to avoid the loop repair you need.

Friends who celebrate your workaholism enable dysregulated Loop 2. They call it dedication. They admire the grind. They never ask what you're running from — and you never have to answer.

Partners who accept your broken promises enable damaged Loop 1. They've learned not to count on you. They've adjusted their expectations. The low bar means you never have to rebuild trust because no one's asking you to.

Social circles that mock ambition enable Loop 2 avoidance. They frame stagnation as wisdom, comfort as enlightenment.[1] You never have to face the discomfort of growth because everyone around you has agreed it's not necessary.

Communities that stay busy with activity but never produce impact enable the appearance of Loop 3 without the reality. Lots of meetings. Lots of intention. No actual contribution. The motion substitutes for meaning.

Enabling relationships feel supportive. They feel accepting. They're environments optimized for staying stuck.

This raises a hard question.

What happens to your relationships when you start repairing your loops?

The honest answer: some of them won't survive.

If a relationship was built on complementary dysfunction — if it required your broken loop to function — then fixing your loop changes the terms. The helper who needs you broken will resist your growth. The partner who enabled your avoidance will be uncomfortable with your new demands on yourself. The friend group that celebrated your workaholism will feel judged by your new boundaries.

This isn't failure. This is structural reality. Some relationships are only stable because both people are stuck. Movement by either person destabilizes the system.

Not all relationships work this way. Some will flex. Some will grow alongside you. Some will be relieved — they were waiting for you to change, hoping you would, ready to meet you there.

But some won't. And pretending otherwise sets you up for surprise when repair creates relational friction.

How to navigate this.

First: repair your own loops regardless of relational consequences. Your foundation is not negotiable. If a relationship requires you to stay broken, that relationship is not serving you — no matter how much it feels like it is.

This doesn't mean abandoning relationships the moment they feel difficult. It means not sacrificing your repair to preserve relational comfort.

Second: notice which relationships support repair and which enable avoidance. This is diagnostic information. The relationships that make growth easier are assets. The relationships that make growth harder are costs. You don't have to cut every costly relationship immediately — but you do need to see clearly what each one is.

Third: expect resistance when you change. People who knew you one way will be disoriented when you become another way. Some will adjust. Some will push back. Some will try to pull you back to the old pattern, not out of malice but out of their own need for stability.

Your job is to keep repairing anyway. Their adjustment is their work, not yours.

Fourth: find people who are also repairing. Environments matter. If you're surrounded by people actively working on their own loops, your repair is supported by contagion instead of undermined by it. The people around you normalize growth instead of stagnation, follow-through instead of negotiation, meaning instead of cynicism.

This might mean seeking new relationships. It might mean deepening certain existing ones while letting others fade. It might mean joining contexts — communities, groups, collaborations — where the relational environment supports than resists the person you're becoming.

The relational dimension doesn't change the loops. It changes the terrain.

The loops still work the same way. They still break the same way. The repair protocols don't change based on who you're in relationship with.

But the difficulty of repair changes. The resistance you face changes. The likelihood of sustaining change changes.

Humans are social. The people around you shape what feels possible. If everyone around you is stuck, staying stuck feels normal. If everyone around you is growing, growing feels normal.

You can't fully control this. You can influence it. By choosing, where possible, to spend time with people whose loop patterns support yours than undermine them. By recognizing when a relationship is enabling your dysfunction. By being willing to let relationships change — or end — when your repair requires it.

One final note.

Repairing your loops will make you a better person to be in relationship with.

Stable Loop 1 means you keep your commitments — to partners, to friends, to family. They can rely on you. That's a gift.

Regulated Loop 2 means you're not using relationships as fuel for achievement or avoidance of it. You can be present without always needing to produce. That's a gift.

Functioning Loop 3 means you can contribute without collapsing, serve without martyrdom, care without self-abandonment. That's a gift.

Therapy without action is rehearsing your reasons. The nervous system doesn't update from conversation. It updates from consequence. Relationships don't update from understanding either. They update from changed behavior.

The relationships that survive your repair—and the new ones you build from a solid foundation—will be better than what came before. Not because you found better people. Because you became someone capable of building something real.

That's what loop repair makes possible. Not a better internal life. A better relational one.

But the repair comes first. You can't give what you don't have. You can't build stable relationships from an unstable foundation.

When your repair creates relational friction

You're rebuilding your loops. Your partner, friend, or family member isn't. Their dysfunction is creating drag on your repair. What do you do?

You can't force them to change. But you can act unilaterally in ways that protect your repair without requiring their participation.

First: Hold your boundaries without explaining them to death.

When you start keeping promises to yourself, the people who benefited from your broken promises will resist. They'll question. They'll push back. They'll accuse you of changing in ways that aren't convenient for them.

Don't justify. Don't over-explain. State the boundary once, clearly, then hold it through action. "I'm not available after 9pm anymore." "I won't be taking on that responsibility." "I need this time for myself."

The boundary doesn't require their agreement. It requires your consistency.

Second: Stop compensating for their loop dysfunction.

If their Loop 1 is broken—if they chronically don't follow through—stop structuring your life around their unreliability. Make plans that don't depend on them. Build systems that function whether they show up or not. Let natural consequences land instead of buffering them.

If their Loop 2 is dysregulated—if they can't stop working or won't start growing—stop enabling it. Don't manage the household solo while they work 80-hour weeks. Don't protect them from the relational cost of their avoidance. The dysfunction continues because someone else is absorbing the cost.

If their Loop 3 is premature or starved—if they're martyring themselves or cynical about everything—stop participating in the pattern. Don't be the audience for martyrdom stories. Don't validate cynicism as wisdom. Refuse the role their dysfunction needs you to play.

Third: Rebuild your life as if the relationship might not change.

This is the hardest one. You want them to change. You're hoping your change will inspire theirs. It might. It might not.

Build the life that works even if they stay stuck. Develop relationships outside this one. Create meaning that doesn't depend on their participation. Repair your loops regardless of whether they repair theirs.

If they eventually change, you'll have a foundation to build with. If they don't, you'll have a life that functions anyway.

. . .

Fourth: Know when the relationship is unsalvageable.

Some relationships survive loop repair. Some don't. If the relationship was built on mutual dysfunction—if it required your broken loops to function—your repair changes the terms fundamentally.

You'll know it's unsalvageable when:

- Your boundaries are treated as attacks rather than information
- Their resistance escalates as your repair progresses
- The relationship only works when you're broken
- Staying requires abandoning the repair

If that's true, the choice becomes clear. Not easy. Clear. The relationship costs more than it provides. The repair matters more than the relationship.

This doesn't mean abandoning people at the first sign of friction. It means recognizing the difference between temporary adjustment and permanent incompatibility.

Some people will meet you where you're going. Some won't. Your job is to keep going either way.

Fix your loops. The relationships will follow.

PART FOUR
LOOP REPAIR PROTOCOLS

CHAPTER 9
REBUILDING SELF-TRUST

"Trust rebuilds one kept promise at a time. Not through grand gestures—through repetition."

This is where repair begins.
    Not because Loop 1 is the most important loop. Because it's the foundation. Everything else depends on it. You can't regulate growth if you can't keep commitments to yourself. You can't build meaning if you can't show up consistently.

If your diagnosis pointed to Loop 1, this chapter is your starting point.

If multiple loops are broken, this chapter is still your starting point.

The foundation comes first.

The repair principle is simple.

Self-trust is rebuilt through kept promises. Small ones. Accumulated over time.

Not grand commitments. Not dramatic transformations. Not "new year, new me" overhauls that collapse by January 15th.

Small promises. Kept promises. Visible evidence that your word means something.

This is counterintuitive. When the foundation is cracked, the instinct is to fix it with something big. A complete life restructure. A radical commitment. Finally getting serious.

That instinct is wrong. It's the same instinct that broke the foundation in the first place. Big promises from someone whose promises don't stick add another failure to the record. The system registers the ambition, then registers the collapse, then trusts you even less.

The repair path is smaller. Unglamorous. Almost embarrassingly modest.

That's why it works.

Here's the mechanism.

Your system tracks what you do, not what you intend. Every kept promise is a data point. Every broken promise is a data point. The system is always updating, always adjusting its model of who you are based on evidence.

Right now, if Loop 1 is broken, the evidence is against you. Years of broken promises, abandoned commitments, negotiations that eroded your word. The system has learned not to believe you.

Reversing this requires new evidence. Enough new evidence to outweigh the old. This doesn't happen overnight. It happens through repetition — kept promise after kept promise, day after day, until the weight of new evidence shifts the balance.

The promises must be small enough to keep. If your system doesn't believe you can keep it, it won't invest in the intention. And if it doesn't invest, you're less likely to follow through. Small promises bypass this resistance. They're believable. The system might not trust you to transform your life, but it might trust you to drink a glass of water when you wake up.

Start there.

. . .

The First Seven Days.

This is a starter protocol. Not a permanent practice — a reset. A way to begin accumulating evidence when the deficit is large.

Day 1-7: One promise. One promise only.

Choose something small. Something you can do in under two minutes. Something that requires almost no willpower, no special conditions, no cooperation from anyone else.

Examples:

- Drink a glass of water when you wake up
- Make your bed before leaving the room
- Put your phone in a specific location when you get home
- Write one sentence in a notebook before sleep

Not all of these. One of them. Or something else equally small.

Make the promise explicit. Say it out loud or write it down: "For the next seven days, I will [specific action] every day."

Then do it. Every day. No exceptions. No negotiations. No "I'll do it twice tomorrow."

Seven days. One promise. Complete follow-through.

Why this works.

The promise is small enough that failure is almost impossible. This matters because what you're building isn't the habit itself — it's the evidence that you keep your word.

The nervous system doesn't distinguish between big and small promises when it comes to trust. A kept small promise registers as: "This person does what they say." A broken small promise registers as: "This person doesn't do what they say." The size is irrelevant. The follow-through is everything.

After seven days of complete follow-through, something subtle shifts. Not transformation. Not confidence. Just a small data point in the other direction. A piece of evidence that suggests maybe, possibly, your word means something.

That's enough to build on.

Week Two and Beyond.

After the first seven days, you have options.

Option A: Keep the same promise, extend another week. If it's working, if the follow-through is clean, there's value in extending. More evidence. Deeper groove.

Option B: Add a second small promise. Now you're keeping two. Still small. Still under two minutes each. But the evidence is accumulating faster.

Option C: Slightly increase the difficulty of the first promise. Make your bed and put away one item of clothing. Drink water and do three stretches. A modest expansion of what you're proving you can do.

Do not jump to large promises. The temptation will come. After a week or two of follow-through, the old pattern will whisper: "See? You've got this. Time to go big."

That's the pattern that broke you. Don't listen to it.

Stay small. Stay consistent. Let the evidence accumulate slowly. Trust is rebuilt in increments, not leaps.

The Daily Practice.

Once you're past the initial reset, self-trust repair becomes a daily practice. Not a dramatic intervention — a quiet discipline.

One kept promise per day. Minimum. This is the floor, not the ceiling. Some days you'll keep many promises. But even on the hardest days, there's one promise you make to yourself and keep.

Visible evidence. The promise must produce something you can see. A checked box. A completed task. A physical change in your environment. Something that proves, to the part of you that tracks these things, that the promise was kept.

Vague promises produce vague evidence. "I'll be more productive" — when did you succeed? "I'll take better care of myself" — how do you know you did it? These aren't promises. They're wishes. And wishes don't rebuild trust.

Specific promises produce clear evidence. "I will close my laptop by 10pm." Either you did or you didn't. "I will eat one vegetable at lunch." Verifiable. "I will respond to that email before noon." Binary.

No self-narration. This is important. Don't tell yourself stories about what keeping the promise means. Don't celebrate excessively. Don't construct a narrative of transformation.

Just do the thing. Register that you did it. Move on.

The narration is where the old pattern hides. It wants to turn one kept promise into evidence of a new you, a changed identity, proof that you've finally figured it out. This inflation sets you up for a fall. When the inevitable slip happens, the narrative collapses, and you're worse off than before.

Keep the promise. Note the evidence. That's it.

What Counts as a Promise.

Not everything is a promise. The distinction matters.

A promise is a specific commitment to yourself about a specific action in a specific timeframe. "I will do X by Y."

Not a promise:

- "I should exercise more" (no specific action, no timeframe)
- "I'm going to be better about sleep" (vague, unmeasurable)
- "I need to call my mother" (intention, not commitment)

A promise:

- I will walk for 10 minutes after lunch today"
- I will be in bed by 11pm tonight"
- "I will call my mother on Sunday at 2pm"

The specificity matters because it creates accountability. Vague intentions give you infinite room to negotiate, redefine, or declare partial success. Specific promises are binary. You either kept them or you didn't.

This is uncomfortable. That's the point. The discomfort of clear accountability is what makes the kept promise meaningful.

Anti-Patterns.

These are the ways people sabotage Loop 1 repair while feeling like they're making progress.

Too many promises. You're excited. You want to rebuild fast. So you make five promises, then ten, then twenty. You're setting up a system where failure is inevitable. When it comes, you'll have more evidence against yourself than when you started.

One promise. Then two. Build slowly.

Promises too large. "I'll work out every day for an hour." If you haven't been working out at all, this is not repair — it's the same grandiose pattern that broke the loop. The system doesn't believe you. And it's right not to believe you.

Start embarrassingly small. Expand gradually.

Negotiation after the fact. You promised to be in bed by 11. At 10:45, you're in the middle of something. The negotiation starts: "11:15 is basically 11. I'll make it up tomorrow. This doesn't count."

Yes, it counts. Every negotiation counts. The system is watching. Every time you renegotiate a promise with yourself, you're teaching it that your word is flexible. That's the opposite of repair.

Using external accountability as a crutch. There's a place for external accountability. But if you can only keep promises when someone else is watching, you haven't rebuilt self-trust — you've built dependency.

The goal is internal accountability. Keeping promises because you said you would. Not because someone will be disappointed. Not because there are consequences. Because your word means something to you.

Treating slips as total failure. You will slip. Not might — will. The practice isn't perfect compliance. It's consistent return.

When you break a promise, the old pattern wants you to catastrophize. "See? You can't do this. You'll never change. Why bother?"

That's the voice of the broken loop defending itself.

The correct response to a slip: Notice it. Don't narrate it. Return to the practice tomorrow. One slip doesn't erase the evidence you've accumulated. It's one data point among many.

When This Isn't Working.

Sometimes people do the practice correctly and nothing shifts. They keep small promises for weeks, and the internal experience doesn't change. The self-trust doesn't rebuild.

This usually means one of three things.

The promises are too easy. If keeping the promise requires zero effort, it might not register as meaningful evidence. There needs to be at least some friction — something that makes the follow-through feel like a choice than an inevitability.

Try slightly increasing the difficulty. Not dramatically. Just enough that keeping the promise requires showing up.

You're keeping promises but not registering them. Some people keep their word all day and never notice. The evidence accumulates but isn't integrated. They need to explicitly mark the kept promise — write it down, check a box, say it out loud. Make the evidence visible to yourself.

Loop 1 isn't the broken loop. This happens. The diagnosis seemed right, but the repair isn't landing. The problem might be elsewhere — dysregulated Loop 2, starved Loop 3, or something outside the loop model entirely (trauma, mental health conditions, medical issues).

Here's the troubleshooting sequence:

After 2 weeks of consistent practice with no shift:

Check promise size. Are you making promises you can keep, or promises you should be able to keep? There's a difference. "I'll drink water when I wake up" is a promise you can keep. "I'll work out for an hour every day" might be a promise you should be able to keep—but if you haven't been working out at all, your system doesn't believe you.

Scale down. Make the promise smaller. Embarrassingly small if necessary. The size doesn't matter. The kept promise does.

After 4 weeks of consistent practice with no shift:

Check visibility. Is the evidence of kept promises actually visible to you, or are you keeping promises and not registering them?

Some people do the action but don't mark it as evidence. They make the bed but don't acknowledge to themselves that they did what they said they would do. The loop needs visible confirmation. Write it down. Check a box. Say it out loud. Make the evidence impossible to miss.

Also check: Are you keeping the same promise, or are you switching promises every few days? Consistency matters. One promise, kept daily, builds more trust than five promises kept sporadically.

After 6 weeks of consistent practice with no shift:

Reconsider the diagnosis. If you've been making small promises, keeping them consistently, making the evidence visible, and your system still isn't updating—you might not have a Loop 1 problem. The issue might be Loop 2 or Loop 3 dysfunction presenting as Loop 1 symptoms.

Or the issue might exceed the book's scope. If Loop 1 repair protocol genuinely applied for six weeks produces zero progress, that's a signal. Not moral failure—diagnostic information. Time to seek professional assessment. Chapter 16 addresses this directly.

After 8 weeks:

If you've applied the protocol correctly and consistently for eight weeks with zero subjective change—if the internal experience of self-trust hasn't shifted at all—something else is blocking the repair. This doesn't mean the model is wrong. It means your situation requires tools this book doesn't provide.

The appropriate next step is professional evaluation. The protocol works for most people with straightforward Loop 1 dysfunction. If it's not working for you, that's information—not about your character, but about what your situation requires.

The Endpoint.

What does repaired self-trust feel like?

Not permanent motivation. Not constant confidence. Not the disappearance of all internal negotiation.

It feels like: your word means something. When you say you'll do something, there's an expectation — from yourself — that you'll do it. The negotiation might still arise, but it doesn't win by default. The intention has weight.

It feels like: the gap between knowing and doing is smaller. Not gone — smaller. The things you know you should do, you're more likely to do. Not perfectly. More likely.

It feels like: a quiet solidity. Not loud confidence. Quiet. You've been keeping your word. You know it. The system knows it. That knowledge changes how you move through the world.

This doesn't happen in a week. It happens over months. Sometimes longer. The damage took years to accumulate. The repair takes time too.

But it's real. And once it's there, everything else becomes possible.

The foundation is where everything else is built.

Rebuild it slowly. Rebuild it right.

CHAPTER 10
REGULATING GROWTH

"Growth without boundaries is cancer. It expands until it kills the host."

Loop 2 breaks in two directions.

It can run too hard — consuming identity, making rest impossible, turning achievement into the only source of worth. Or it can be abandoned — avoided under sophisticated disguises, comfort mistaken for wisdom, stagnation dressed as enlightenment.

Repair looks different depending on which direction you've broken.

If you can't stop, this chapter is about learning to bound growth — to push without being consumed.

If you've stopped entirely, this chapter is about re-entering discomfort — deliberately, sustainably, without the patterns that made you avoid it in the first place.

Both repairs require the same foundation: Loop 1 must be functional first. If you can't keep promises to yourself, you can't regulate growth or sustain deliberate discomfort. Build the foundation before you work on this loop.

. . .

For the person who can't stop.

Your problem isn't lack of growth. It's growth without boundaries. The loop runs and runs, extracting everything, giving nothing back. Achievement has become identity. Output has become worth. Rest has become threat.

The repair isn't to stop growing. It's to make growth serve you instead of consume you.

This requires three things: bounded effort, enforced recovery, and identity separation.

Bounded effort.

Growth without limits is cancer. It expands until it kills the host. You need limits — not as punishment, but as protection.

Define the container. What are the actual boundaries of your work? Not "as much as it takes" — that's not a boundary. Actual limits. Hours per day. Days per week. Projects at a time.

This feels dangerous. You've been told — or told yourself — that limits are for people who don't want it enough. That boundaries are for the uncommitted. That real achievers push through.

That story is what broke you.

Limits aren't the opposite of achievement. They're what makes achievement sustainable. The person who works sixteen hours today and burns out in six months accomplishes less than the person who works eight hours today for the next ten years.

Make the limits specific. "I'll try to work less" is not a limit. "I close my laptop at 7pm" is a limit. "I'll take breaks when I need them" is not a limit. "I take a fifteen-minute break every ninety minutes" is a limit.

Here's what bounded effort looks like in practice:

Example 1: The founder who can't stop
Before: Works 6am-11pm, seven days a week. Laptop always

open. Responds to messages immediately regardless of hour. Family dinners are interrupted. Sleep is negotiable.

Bounded version: Works 8am-6pm Monday-Friday, 9am-1pm Saturday. Laptop stays closed Sunday. Phone on Do Not Disturb from 6pm-8am. Family dinner is non-negotiable—no devices. If something truly urgent happens, it can wait until morning. (It almost never is actually urgent.)

The container is specific. The hours are fixed. The boundaries are binary—either inside the container or outside it. No grey area.

Example 2: The executive who uses achievement to avoid

Before: Accepts every opportunity. Sits on four boards. Mentors eight people. Chairs two committees. Volunteers for additional projects while current projects aren't finished. Rest feels like laziness.

Bounded version: One primary role. One board position. Two mentees maximum. No committee work for the next year. New opportunities get a default "no" unless they replace something existing. One day per week with no meetings—time for strategic thinking, not filling with more tasks.

The limit isn't effort—it's scope. The growth continues, but it's directional rather than diffuse. Quality over quantity. Depth over breadth.

Example 3: The caregiver running Loop 2 through relational over-functioning

Before: Manages everyone's emotions. Solves everyone's problems. Available 24/7 for family crises. Own needs are perpetually deferred. Competence at caregiving has become identity.

Bounded version: Available for genuine emergencies only—defined in advance (medical crisis, safety issue). Non-emergencies get a callback window: "I'll call you back between 7-8pm." Problems that are someone else's to solve stay with them—no rescuing. One evening per week is unavailable for anyone—no exceptions.

The boundary here is responsibility. What's actually yours to carry versus what you've been carrying that belongs to someone else.

The specificity matters because vague limits get negotiated away. Every time. You'll always find a reason why this project is different, why this deadline requires an exception, why the limit doesn't apply today. Specific limits are harder to negotiate. They're binary. You either kept them or you didn't.

Track compliance. Did you stop when you said you would? Did you take the break? Did you stay within the container you set?

If you're not tracking, you're not regulating. You're hoping.

Enforced recovery.

Rest isn't optional. It's part of the system.

The growth loop runs on a cycle: effort, adaptation, capacity increase. But adaptation doesn't happen during the effort. It happens during recovery. Skip the recovery and you skip the adaptation. You're extracting from yourself without letting anything rebuild.

This is how burnout works. It's not too much effort. It's effort without recovery. The system breaks down because it's never allowed to rebuild.

Recovery must be scheduled. If recovery happens "when there's time," it won't happen. There's never time. There's always another task, another project, another thing that seems more urgent than rest.

Schedule recovery like you schedule work. Put it in the calendar. Treat it as non-negotiable.

Recovery must be actual rest. Scrolling your phone isn't recovery. Watching TV while answering emails isn't recovery. Thinking about work while technically not working isn't recovery.

Recovery means the system gets to rebuild. That requires genuine disengagement. Time when you're not producing, not optimizing, not achieving. Time when you're existing.

This will feel unproductive. That's the point. Productivity is the thing you're recovering from.

Recovery must be proportional. Harder effort requires more recovery. A heavy week requires a lighter weekend. A demanding quarter requires actual time off, not a day here and there.

You know how much you've been extracting. Be honest about how much recovery that extraction requires.

Identity separation.

This is the hardest part.

If your identity has fused with your output, then rest feels like self-erasure. Taking a break feels like disappearing. You don't know who you are when you're not producing.

The repair is to rebuild an identity that exists independent of achievement.

Notice what you are beyond output. You have relationships that aren't about what you produce. You have interests that aren't about optimization. You have a body that exists whether or not it's being used as a tool.

These parts of you have been neglected. They haven't disappeared. But they've atrophied because all the attention went to achievement.

Start paying attention to them again. Not as another project to optimize — as parts of yourself that exist whether or not they produce anything.

Practice existing without producing. Spend time doing

nothing useful. Not as a strategy for better productivity later. As practice in being a person who doesn't have to produce to exist.

This will be uncomfortable. The discomfort is diagnostic. It shows how fused your identity has become with output. Sit with the discomfort. Let it be uncomfortable. You don't have to fix it by doing something productive.

Separate worth from output. This is internal work. Noticing when you feel worthless because you didn't accomplish enough. Noticing when you feel valuable only because of what you produced. Catching the equation as it runs and questioning it.

Worth is not output. You knew this as a child, before achievement became the only source of identity. You can know it again.

For the person who's stopped entirely.

Your problem is the opposite. Growth has been abandoned. The discomfort required for development has been avoided. You've built a life where nothing is difficult — and called it wisdom.

The repair isn't to suddenly become an achiever. It's to re-enter discomfort deliberately, sustainably, without the patterns that made you avoid it.

Deliberate discomfort.

Growth requires discomfort. There's no way around this. If you're not uncomfortable, you're not at your edge. If you're not at your edge, you're not growing.

The avoidance pattern says: comfort is the goal. Discomfort is a sign something is wrong. If it's hard, maybe it's not meant to be.

That pattern is stagnation with good marketing.

Choose one area to develop. Not everything at once. One domain where you've been avoiding growth. Maybe it's physical — your body has been neglected. Maybe it's professional —

you've plateaued and stopped pushing. Maybe it's relational — the vulnerability required for deeper connection has been avoided.

Pick one area. Just one.

Enter discomfort deliberately. Find the edge in that area and push into it. Not recklessly — deliberately. Knowing it will be uncomfortable. Choosing the discomfort anyway.

The discomfort is not a sign you're doing it wrong. It's a sign you're doing it right. Growth lives in discomfort. If you're comfortable, you're not growing.

Start small. If you've been avoiding discomfort for a long time, you've lost tolerance for it. Your capacity to handle difficulty has atrophied. Starting with a huge challenge will overwhelm you and reinforce the avoidance pattern.

Start with discomfort you can handle. Then gradually increase. Rebuild the tolerance that avoidance eroded.

Don't spiritualize the avoidance. The mind is clever. It will construct beautiful reasons why growth isn't necessary. Why you're beyond ambition. Why striving is ego. Why you've transcended the need to push.

Sometimes this is true. Often it's cover. The test is simple: Do you have the capability and choose not to use it? Or do you lack the capability and pretend you don't want it?

Transcendence comes after mastery, not instead of it. If you haven't built the competence, you haven't transcended the need for it. You've avoided it.

Skill tracking.

Growth needs feedback. Without it, you can't tell if you're developing or going through the motions.

Define what capability you're building. Be specific. Not "get better at my job" — that's unmeasurable. "Close one additional sale per month." "Run a mile thirty seconds faster." "Have one difficult conversation I've been avoiding."

Specific capability. Measurable progress.

Track the trajectory. Are you improving? The tracking doesn't have to be complicated. A simple log works. Date, what you did, what you noticed.

The point is to create visibility. To see, over time, whether the discomfort is producing development. If it is, keep going. If it isn't, adjust.

Celebrate competence, not effort. The avoidance pattern often disguises itself as effort without results. "I'm trying" becomes a permanent state. Trying isn't growing. Results are growing.

This doesn't mean results have to be huge. Small improvements count. But there have to be actual improvements — actual capability increases that you can point to. Effort that produces nothing is motion.

Anti-patterns for both directions.

These sabotage Loop 2 repair regardless of which direction you've broken.

Using growth to avoid foundation. If Loop 1 is still broken, growth won't land. You'll push and achieve, and none of it will feel like yours. Or you'll re-enter discomfort without the self-trust to sustain it, and collapse back into avoidance.

Fix the foundation first. Growth built on a cracked foundation doesn't hold.

Swinging to the opposite extreme. The workaholic who burns out doesn't need to become someone who never works. The avoider who's stagnated doesn't need to become a relentless achiever.

Regulation isn't about swinging from one extreme to the other. It's about finding the bounded middle — growth that's real but sustainable, effort that's present but not consuming.

Making growth the new identity. "I'm someone who's

working on balance." "I'm someone who's re-entering challenge." These can become identities as rigid as the ones they replaced.

Growth serves identity. It doesn't become identity. If your sense of self depends on the fact that you're growing, you've replaced one fusion with another.

Expecting immediate transformation. Loop 2 regulation takes time. The workaholic won't feel comfortable resting after one weekend off. The avoider won't be comfortable with challenge after one hard workout.

The patterns took years to form. They take time to shift. Expect gradual change, not overnight transformation.

The integrated state.

What does regulated growth look like?

You push — but not past the point of extraction. You seek challenge — but you also recover. You develop capability — but capability isn't all you are. You can work hard and rest fully. You can achieve and be present. You can grow and be content with who you are right now.

Growth serves you. You don't serve growth.

This is the bounded loop. Not the avoidance of growth — the regulation of it. Not the worship of achievement — the appropriate use of it.

Development without consumption. Effort without extraction. Capability that increases without identity that depends on it.

That's the repair. Not perfect balance — functional regulation. Growth in its proper place, serving what matters, stopping when stopping is right.

CHAPTER 11
EARNING MEANING

"Meaning isn't discovered in contemplation. It's built through contribution that costs something."

Loop 3 doesn't get repaired the same way as the others.

Loops 1 and 2 can be worked on directly. You can make promises and keep them. You can enter discomfort and build capability. The actions are concrete, the feedback is immediate, the progress is measurable.

Loop 3 is different. Meaning can't be manufactured through effort alone. It emerges from contribution — but only when the contribution is real, sustained, and built on stable ground.

This chapter addresses both failure modes: meaning starvation (the successful person who feels empty) and premature meaning (the helper who's falling apart). The repairs look different, but they share the same foundation.

You can't work on Loop 3 until Loops 1 and 2 are functional. If you can't trust yourself, your contribution will be erratic. If you can't regulate growth, your service will either consume you or remain ineffective. The sequence matters.

. . .

For the person with meaning starvation.

You've built capability. You've achieved things. By external measures, you've succeeded. And none of it feels like anything.

The problem isn't that you've done too much. It's that everything you've done has been oriented inward — toward your own success, your own advancement, your own accumulation. The growth was real. It never connected to anything beyond itself.

The repair is to begin directing capability outward. Not dramatically. Not by abandoning what you've built. By starting to contribute in ways that matter to something other than your own advancement.

Finding contribution.

Meaning isn't found through contemplation. It's built through action. You don't discover what matters by thinking about it. You discover it by contributing and noticing what lands.

Start where you already are. You don't need to quit your job, move to a new city, or reinvent your life. Contribution can begin within your current context. What do you already know how to do? Who around you could benefit from that capability?

The CEO who feels hollow doesn't need to abandon leadership. They might need to start mentoring someone with no strategic value to them. The professional who's succeeded but feels empty doesn't need a career change. They might need to start using their skills for someone who can't pay for them.

Contribution doesn't require a new life. It requires directing existing capability toward something beyond personal gain.

Contribute without strategic value. This is the test. Can you give something — time, skill, attention — to someone or something that will never benefit you? Not as networking disguised as generosity. Not as resume-building dressed up as service. Actual contribution with no return.

If every act of giving has an angle, you're still running Loop 2. Growth, optimization, accumulation — with a charitable veneer. That's not meaning. That's achievement wearing a different costume.

Meaning requires contribution that costs something and returns nothing except the contribution itself.

Notice what resonates. As you begin contributing, pay attention. Some service will feel like obligation — necessary but draining. Some will feel different — still effortful, but somehow sustaining than depleting.

That difference is information. The contribution that sustains you is pointing toward where your meaning might live. Not as a final answer — as a direction worth exploring.

For the person running premature meaning.

You're already contributing. Maybe too much. You help everyone, you're available constantly, you give and give. And you're falling apart.

The problem isn't that contribution is wrong for you. It's that you're contributing from an empty vessel. The service isn't an expression of abundance — it's a compensation for missing foundation. You're using Loop 3 to avoid Loops 1 and 2.

The repair is counterintuitive: you need to pull back. Not permanently. Not because service is bad. Because your current service is unsustainable, and unsustainable service eventually collapses into no service at all.

If you're depleted to the point where "contribute beyond yourself" sounds impossible, start smaller than you think you should.

Contribution can be five minutes. One email to someone who needs to hear from you. One conversation where you're present instead of performing. One moment of actually listening instead of fixing.

The loop doesn't measure scale. It measures direction. The

question isn't "how much did you give?" It's "did your effort touch something beyond yourself?"

The person recovering from burnout who sends a single thoughtful message to a struggling colleague—that's Loop 3 functioning. Not dramatically. Not heroically. But functioning.

The parent who's exhausted but shows up fully for ten minutes of genuine attention to their child—that's Loop 3. The contribution isn't the length of time. It's the quality of presence.

The professional who's barely holding on but takes five minutes to mentor a junior colleague on one specific thing—that's Loop 3. The impact might seem small. The direction is what matters.

Start there. Five minutes of genuine contribution from actual capacity, not from depletion. That plants the seed. The loop can grow from there. But it has to start with contribution that doesn't require draining an already empty vessel.

As capacity rebuilds—as Loop 1 stabilizes, as Loop 2 regulates—the contribution can deepen. But it doesn't start deep. It starts true. Small, genuine, sustainable contribution beats grand martyrdom every time.

Pulling back without abandoning.

Acknowledge the compensation. Be honest with yourself. Is your helping about helping? Or is it about avoiding your own broken foundation? About having an identity when your self-trust is shattered? About feeling needed when you can't feel solid?

This isn't judgment. It's diagnosis. Knowing why you're overgiving helps you see what needs repair.

Reduce contribution to sustainable levels. What would you be able to give if you were only giving from actual surplus? Not from depletion, not from obligation, not from the desperate need to be needed. From genuine capacity.

That's less than what you're currently giving. Possibly much less. Scale back to that level.

This will feel like failure. Like selfishness. Like abandoning people who need you. Those feelings are the compensation pattern defending itself. They're not accurate assessments of what's required.

Repair the foundation while contributing less. Use the energy you've freed up to work on Loops 1 and 2. Build self-trust. Regulate growth. Become someone whose contribution comes from stability than from need.

This is temporary. Once the foundation is solid, you'll be able to contribute more — and contribute better. But you can't get there by continuing to pour from an empty vessel.

Contribution without applause.

One of the tests of genuine meaning is whether the contribution survives the absence of recognition.

If you're contributing primarily for the appreciation, the acknowledgment, the sense of being seen as generous — that's still Loop 2 dynamics. Achievement, validation, external feedback. The contribution is real, but it's running on the wrong fuel.

Genuine Loop 3 contribution doesn't require applause. The meaning comes from the contribution itself, not from what you get back for it.

Practice anonymous contribution. Give something that no one will know you gave. Help in a way that won't be traced back to you. Contribute where there's no possibility of credit.

This strips away the achievement layer. What remains is the contribution itself — and whether that's enough.

If anonymous contribution feels meaningless, that's diagnostic. The meaning was in the recognition, not in the service. That's not wrong — it's not Loop 3. It's Loop 2 wearing a service costume.

If anonymous contribution feels satisfying — if there's something that lands even without acknowledgment — that's Loop 3 starting to function. The meaning is in the mattering, not in being seen to matter.

Responsibility with boundaries.

Meaning involves responsibility. When you contribute to something, you become accountable for it. People depend on you. Expectations form. The contribution creates obligations.

This is appropriate. It's part of how meaning works. Impact creates responsibility, responsibility deepens service, service generates more meaning.

But responsibility without boundaries becomes martyrdom.

Define what you're responsible for. Be specific. Not "helping everyone" — that's not a responsibility, it's a recipe for collapse. What specifically are you accountable for? To whom? Within what limits?

Clarity about responsibility creates clarity about boundaries. You know what's yours to carry and what isn't. You can give fully within your domain without being consumed by everything outside it.

Protect the boundaries. Once defined, the boundaries need protection. People will ask for more. Circumstances will demand exceptions. The boundary will feel selfish when someone needs what you've decided not to give.

Hold the boundary anyway. Not because you don't care. Because boundary-less service isn't sustainable service. The contribution that burns you out isn't a contribution — it's a slow-motion withdrawal from the capacity to contribute at all.

Let some things not be your responsibility. This is hard for people prone to premature meaning. Everything feels urgent. Everyone needs help. How can you not respond?

You can not respond because you're one person with finite capacity. Because saying yes to everything means doing everything poorly. Because sustainable contribution requires accepting that some problems won't be solved by you.

Your responsibility is bounded. That boundary is what makes the responsibility sustainable.

Matching service to capacity.

Your capacity to contribute is not infinite. It's not even constant. It varies based on your foundation, your energy, your current demands, your season of life.

Service that exceeds capacity isn't generosity. It's extraction wearing a mask.

Know your current capacity. How much can you give right now — not ideally, not at your best, but , in this season? Be honest. Overestimating capacity is how premature meaning collapses into burnout.

Match contribution to that capacity. Not to what you wish your capacity was. Not to what it used to be. Not to what others seem capable of. To what you can , sustainably provide.

This might mean contributing less than you want to. Less than seems needed. Less than you could theoretically give if you ignored your own limits.

That's appropriate. Sustainable contribution that continues for years beats heroic contribution that burns out in months.

Adjust as capacity changes. Your capacity isn't fixed. It increases as foundation stabilizes, as growth regulates, as meaning deepens. What you can sustainably give in five years might be more than what you can sustainably give today.

Let contribution scale with capacity. Not ahead of it.

Anti-patterns.

Service as avoidance. Using contribution to avoid your own broken foundation. Helping others because it's easier than facing yourself. This is compensation, not meaning. The signal: you feel depleted after helping, resentful of those you've helped, or unable to stop even when you're empty.

Meaning as identity. Needing to be the helper, the giver, the one who cares. When meaning becomes identity, losing the service feels like losing yourself. That's fusion, not function. The signal: you can't imagine who you'd be if you stopped helping.

Contribution without capability. Wanting to help but lacking the competence to help. Good intentions without the skill to execute them. This is sentiment, not service. Build capability first. The signal: your help doesn't help. People aren't better off for your involvement.

Boundary-less giving. Saying yes to everything. Being available constantly. Treating your own limits as selfishness. This produces martyrdom, resentment, and eventual collapse — not sustainable meaning. The signal: you give until you crash, recover, then do it again.

Waiting for perfect conditions. "I'll contribute when I have more time, more money, more stability." Perfect conditions don't arrive. Contribution can start small, now, with what you have. The signal: years pass without actual service, only planning for future service.

What functional meaning looks like.

You contribute — but not from depletion. The giving comes from surplus, from capability, from a stable foundation that can sustain the service.

You're responsible — but bounded. You know what's yours to carry. You carry it fully. You let go of what isn't yours.

You care — but not at the cost of yourself. The service doesn't require self-abandonment. The meaning doesn't depend on burning out.

Effort connects to something beyond itself. The work has direction. The contribution matters to someone other than you. There's a reason to sustain the effort that isn't personal gain.

This produces a particular kind of stability. Not the stability of having achieved enough. The stability of mattering. Of being connected to something that will continue beyond your own comfort and survival.

That's meaning. Not found. Earned. Through contribution that's real, sustained, and built on ground that can hold it.

PART FIVE
LOOP SWITCHING

CHAPTER 12
THE ADULT SKILL NO ONE TEACHES

"Most people destroy themselves by running yesterday's loop in today's conditions."

You now know the three loops. You know how they work, how they break, how to repair them.

But knowing each loop isn't enough. The real skill is knowing which loop to run today.

This is loop switching — the capacity to read your current situation accurately and respond with the right system. To stabilize when stabilization is needed. To push when pushing is right. To serve when service is called for. To stop when stopping is the answer.

No one teaches this. Schools don't cover it. Parents rarely model it. The culture pushes one loop or another — hustle culture glorifies Loop 2, spiritual culture glorifies Loop 3, therapy culture focuses on Loop 1 — but almost no one teaches the integration.

Yet this is what adult functioning requires. Not running one loop perfectly. Running all three appropriately, switching between them as conditions demand.

. . .

The problem with single-loop focus.

Most people get stuck because they're running yesterday's loop in today's conditions.

The person who needed to rebuild self-trust years ago did the work. Loop 1 is stable now. But they're still treating every situation as a foundation problem. Still making micro-promises when what's needed is bold action. Still stabilizing when they should be pushing.

The person who developed capability through years of deliberate discomfort has competence now. Loop 2 did its job. But they're still grinding, still pushing, still treating every situation as a growth opportunity. They don't need more capability. They need to direct it somewhere that matters.

The person who found meaning through service has contribution now. Loop 3 is running. But they're serving when they should be resting. Giving when they're depleted. They don't need more meaning. They need to rebuild the foundation that service has eroded.

The loops aren't meant to run constantly. They're meant to run when they're needed. The skill is reading the signal and responding with the right loop.

Signals that Loop 1 needs attention.

You're negotiating with yourself constantly. Every commitment becomes a debate. Every intention gets bargained down. The internal conversation is exhausting before any action even happens.

Promises aren't landing. You make commitments — to yourself or others — and they don't mean anything. There's no weight behind them. You know, before you even finish speaking, that follow-through is unlikely.

The gap between knowing and doing is wide. You understand what needs to happen. You can explain it clearly. You can't seem to do it. The knowing and the doing feel like different countries.

Exhaustion without accomplishment. You're tired, but you haven't done anything. The fatigue comes from fighting yourself, not from productive effort.

Shame without crisis. Nothing dramatic has happened. But there's a low-grade shame humming in the background. The quiet knowledge that you're not living according to your own word.

When these signals are present, stop what you're doing and return to Loop 1. Small promises. Visible evidence. Rebuild the foundation before attempting anything else.

Signals that Loop 2 needs attention.

You're stagnating. Nothing is difficult anymore. You've built a comfortable life where challenge is absent. Growth has stopped, and you've told yourself a story about why that's okay.

Capability is needed but missing. There's something you want to do or need to do, and you can't do it. Not because of self-trust issues — because you lack the skill. The gap is competence, not commitment.

You're coasting on old development. The skills you have were built years ago. You've been running on that foundation without adding to it. The world has moved, and your capabilities haven't kept pace.

Comfort has become the goal. Every decision optimizes for ease. Discomfort is avoided systematically. The avoidance has become so habitual you don't notice it anymore.

You're bored but not admitting it. There's a flatness to daily life. Nothing is challenging enough to engage you fully. You're going through motions that used to mean something.

When these signals are present, it's time to engage Loop 2. Find your edge. Enter deliberate discomfort. Build capability you don't currently have.

· · ·

Signals that Loop 3 needs attention.

Achievement feels empty. You're accomplishing things, but they don't land. The wins happen and then evaporate. There's no satisfaction that persists.

The "why bother" question is getting louder. It used to be background noise. Now it's harder to ignore. You're struggling to find reasons for effort beyond immediate necessity.

Everything is about you. When you examine your efforts honestly, they all serve your own advancement. There's no contribution to anything beyond yourself. No service that doesn't have an angle.

Success hasn't satisfied. You've achieved what you set out to achieve. You expected to feel different. You don't. The goalpost moved, or the victory was hollow, or something is missing that achievement can't provide.

Cynicism is creeping in. You're starting to believe that meaning is a fantasy. That everyone is self-interested. That caring about anything larger than yourself is naive. This feels like wisdom. It's starvation.

When these signals are present, it's time to engage Loop 3. Find contribution. Direct capability toward something beyond yourself. Build meaning through service.

Signals that you need to stop.

Not every signal calls for a different loop. Sometimes the signal is: stop running loops altogether.

You're depleted. Not tired from a hard day — depleted at a systemic level. The tank is empty. Running any loop from this state will make things worse.

You're forcing. The effort feels like grinding against resistance. Not the productive resistance of growth — the unproductive resistance of a system that needs rest, not more input.

You're ignoring body signals. Pain, exhaustion, illness — signals that something needs to stop. You're overriding these signals with willpower. This is extraction, not function.

Everything feels like obligation. Loop 1 promises feel like chores. Loop 2 growth feels like punishment. Loop 3 contribution feels like burden. The loops aren't energising anything. They're more weight.

Recovery keeps getting postponed. There's always a reason why rest can happen later. Later never comes. The debt accumulates.

When these signals are present, stop. Not switch loops — stop. Rest. Recover. Let the system rebuild. The loops will still be there when you have capacity to run them.

The switching skill in practice.

How does this work day to day?

Morning assessment. Before you start, check in. What's needed today? Not what's on the to-do list — what does your current state require? If you're negotiating with yourself before your feet hit the floor, that's a Loop 1 signal. If you're avoiding something challenging, that's a Loop 2 signal. If everything feels pointless, that's a Loop 3 signal. If everything feels heavy, maybe you need to stop.

Honest diagnosis, not aspirational. The skill requires honesty about what's happening, not what you wish were happening. You might want to be in Loop 3, serving something meaningful. But if you can't keep a simple promise to yourself, you're not ready for that. You might want to be done with Loop 1 work. But if the signals are present, the foundation still needs attention.

Right-sized response. When you identify which loop needs attention, respond appropriately. If Loop 1 is calling, make one small promise and keep it. Don't make twenty. If Loop 2 is calling, find one edge to push against. Don't restructure your entire life. If Loop 3 is calling, make one contribution. Don't try to save the world by Thursday.

Willingness to switch mid-stream. Conditions change. You might start the day in Loop 2 mode, pushing on a project. Halfway through, you notice you're negotiating with yourself about every small step. That's a Loop 1 signal. Switching isn't failure — it's responsiveness. Staying in the wrong loop because you started there is the mistake.

Rhythm over rigidity. The loops don't need equal time. Some seasons are primarily Loop 1 seasons — stabilising after disruption. Some are primarily Loop 2 seasons — building capability for a new challenge. Some are primarily Loop 3 seasons — contributing from accumulated capacity. The rhythm varies. The skill is reading what's needed now, not applying a fixed formula.

What it looks like when it's working.

A person with integrated loops doesn't look superhuman. They look coherent.

They push when pushing is called for — but they know when to stop. They don't grind past the point of extraction. They don't rest when what's needed is effort.

They serve when service is needed — but not from depletion. Their contribution comes from actual capacity. When the capacity isn't there, they rebuild it before giving more away.

They keep their word — not perfectly, but consistently. When they say they'll do something, it means something. To themselves and to others.

They don't run the same loop regardless of conditions. They read the situation. They respond appropriately. They switch when switching is required.

This produces a particular quality of life. Not ease — coherence. The feeling that effort is going where effort should go. That rest happens when rest is needed. That growth serves purpose and purpose is built on stable ground.

It's not about optimization. It's not about maximization. It's about fit — the right loop for the right situation, applied in the right proportion.

The ongoing practice.

Loop switching isn't a skill you master once. It's an ongoing practice.

Conditions change. Life stages shift. What needed your attention last year might not need it this year. The loop that was primary for a decade might need to become secondary. The loop you neglected might start demanding focus.

The practice is: keep reading the signals. Keep responding honestly. Keep switching when switching is required.

This means regular assessment. Not obsessive — regular. Checking in with yourself: What's needed here? Which loop is calling? Am I running yesterday's loop in today's conditions?

It means accepting imperfection. You'll read signals wrong sometimes. You'll stay in a loop too long or switch too quickly. The practice isn't perfect accuracy. It's continued attention and willingness to adjust.

It means trusting the system. The system is already live. The signals are already present. You don't have to manufacture the information. You have to receive it and respond.

This is adult functioning.

Not running one loop perfectly. Not finding the one answer that solves everything. Not optimizing yourself into a static ideal state.

Adult functioning isn't static. It's noticing what changed—and responding before damage sets in.

Stabilize when the foundation is shaky. Push when growth is needed. Serve when contribution is called for. Stop when rest is required.

That's the skill. Simple to state. Challenging to execute. Worth practicing for a lifetime.

You're not starting this. You're noticing it. The signals are already present. The only question is whether you're listening — and whether you're willing to respond with what's needed, than what you wish were needed.

That's loop switching. That's integration. That's what no one teaches but everyone requires.

PART SIX
LOOPS ACROSS A LIFETIME

CHAPTER 13
LOOPS IN YOUR 20S AND 30S

"The foundation you build—or fail to build—in your twenties is what you'll stand on at forty."

The loops express differently across a lifetime.

What demands attention at twenty-five is not what demands attention at forty-five. The loop that should be primary in your thirties might need to become secondary in your fifties. The mistake that's forgivable at one stage becomes catastrophic at another.

This isn't about rigid life stages or developmental milestones. It's about recognizing that the same loops interact with different conditions at different points in life — and understanding what that means for how you run them.

This chapter covers the twenties and thirties. The foundation-building years. The years where the patterns that will either serve or destroy you get established.

Get this stage right, and you have something to build on. Get it wrong, and you'll spend the next decades repairing what could have been built properly the first time.

. . .

What's being demanded.

In your twenties and thirties, life is making specific demands whether you recognize them or not.

Loop 1 is being established. This is when self-trust either gets built or gets broken. The habits you form now — the relationship between your word and your action — will be your default for decades. If you learn to keep promises to yourself in this period, you'll have a foundation to build on. If you learn to negotiate, defer, and abandon your commitments, you'll spend your forties trying to repair what your twenties broke.

The stakes feel low. You can miss a workout, break a commitment, abandon a project — and nothing dramatic happens. Tomorrow comes anyway. This apparent lack of consequence is deceptive. The loop is registering every failure. The pattern is forming. The foundation is cracking, quietly, invisibly, while you assume there's always more time.

Loop 2 is primary. This is the growth decade (or two). The time when capability gets built. Skills, competencies, earning power, professional identity — they're all being established now. The discomfort you're willing to enter, the edges you're willing to push, the capabilities you're willing to build — these determine what you'll have to work with for the rest of your life.

This doesn't mean frantic achievement. It means deliberate development. Building competence in areas that matter. Acquiring skills that will compound. Entering the discomfort required for growth than avoiding it under the guise of work-life balance or self-care.

Loop 3 is forming but not dominant. Meaning in this stage is usually nascent. You're beginning to ask what matters, beginning to sense that achievement alone might not be enough. But the full weight of the meaning question hasn't landed yet. You have the luxury of deferring it — a luxury that will expire.

The danger isn't that you haven't found your purpose. The danger is that you're so absorbed in Loop 1 and Loop 2 that you don't notice Loop 3 exists. You build capability without direction. You grow without asking what the growth is for. Then you wake up at forty-two with a successful life that means nothing.

What typically breaks.

Self-trust erodes through small betrayals. No one sets out to destroy their foundation. It happens through a thousand small negotiations. The alarm that gets snoozed. The commitment that gets pushed to tomorrow. The promise that gets quietly abandoned when no one's watching.

In your twenties, this feels harmless. You have energy. You have time. You can compensate. But each small betrayal is a data point. The pattern is forming. By your early thirties, many people discover that their self-trust has been hollowed out without them noticing. They know what to do, they intend to do it, and somehow they can't make themselves do it. The foundation cracked years ago. They're now feeling the instability.

Growth gets misdirected. The twenties and thirties often produce growth in the wrong directions. You develop capabilities that the market rewards rather than capabilities that matter to you. You build skills for careers you fell into rather than careers you chose. You push edges that impress others than edges that develop you.

This isn't wasted effort — capability is capability. But it's inefficient. You arrive at forty with a skill set optimized for a life you don't want. The growth happened. It didn't go anywhere useful.

Identity fuses with achievement too early. The achievers in this age bracket are especially at risk. They start winning — grades, jobs, promotions, recognition — and the winning feels good. So they optimize for more winning. Somewhere in the process, their identity fuses with their output. They become what they produce.

This fusion won't feel like a problem for years. It will feel like success. But it's setting up a collapse. When the achievement slows down — as it eventually must — they'll have no identity to fall back on. They'll have built a self that only exists while producing.

Meaning gets indefinitely deferred. "I'll figure out what matters after I've built enough." "I'll contribute once I'm more established." "Purpose comes later, once I've handled the practical stuff."

These deferrals are reasonable in isolation. They're catastrophic in accumulation. You can defer meaning for a year, maybe five. Defer it for fifteen and you wake up in midlife having built a successful life with no answer to the question of why any of it matters.

The common mistakes.

Mistake 1: Treating Loop 1 as optional.

You're young. You have energy. You can power through the internal resistance. So you don't bother building self-trust — you override its absence with willpower.

This works until it doesn't. The willpower depletes. The resistance grows. By your mid-thirties, you're fighting yourself constantly, exhausted before you begin, wondering why everything feels so hard.

The mistake was ignoring the foundation. The cost comes due later.

Mistake 2: Running Loop 2 without boundaries from the start.

You throw yourself into growth. You work the long hours. You say yes to everything. You treat your body as a tool and your relationships as obstacles. You tell yourself it's temporary — you'll rest when you've made it.

But the pattern is forming. The loop is learning how to run. By the time you realize you need boundaries, you've spent a decade training yourself to ignore them. The dysregulation isn't a phase. It's an identity.

Mistake 3: Borrowing meaning instead of building it.

You adopt someone else's answer to the meaning question. Your parents' values. Your culture's metrics. Your peer group's definition of success. It's easier than building your own — and in your twenties, borrowed meaning can feel indistinguishable from the real thing.

The problem emerges later. Borrowed meaning doesn't hold under pressure. It doesn't sustain effort through difficulty. It collapses when circumstances change or when the people you borrowed it from aren't around to reinforce it.

You can't borrow meaning forever. At some point, you have to earn your own.

Mistake 4: Assuming there's time.

This is the meta-mistake that enables all the others. You assume the twenties and thirties are practice. That the real game starts later. That you can defer the foundation work, the growth direction, the meaning question — and handle them all when you're older and wiser.

There is time. But less than you think. And the patterns you're forming now will be the patterns you have to work with or work against for the rest of your life.

The twenties and thirties aren't practice. They're when the defaults get set.

Common mistakes (20s and 30s):

- **Treating Loop 1 as optional.** "I'll get disciplined once life stabilizes." Life doesn't stabilize. The chaos you're navigating now is training ground. Build self-trust in the mess, or you'll arrive at 40 still negotiating with yourself.
- **Assuming energy compensates for structure.** You can override broken self-trust with sheer energy in your twenties. By your mid-thirties, the compensation stops

working. The cracks you're covering now will become chasms later.
- **Chasing achievement without asking what it's for.** You're building capability in whatever direction pays or impresses. Ten years from now, you'll have a skill set optimized for a life you don't want. Direction matters more than speed.
- **Deferring meaning indefinitely.** "I'll figure out what matters after I'm established." After is never. The meaning question doesn't get easier with time. It gets more urgent and more costly to ignore.
- **Borrowing someone else's answers.** Your parents' values. Your culture's metrics. Your peer group's definition of success. Borrowed meaning works until it doesn't. When it collapses—and it will—you'll have to build your own from scratch. Better to start now.

What helps.

Build Loop 1 now, while it's easy. Self-trust is easier to build than to repair. If you establish the pattern now — promises made, promises kept — you'll have a foundation that serves you for decades. If you wait until the pattern is broken, you'll spend years undoing damage instead of building capacity.

This doesn't require perfection. It requires attention. Notice when you're negotiating with yourself. Notice when your word is becoming meaningless. Catch the erosion early. Build the foundation while building it is still straightforward.

Start small. One kept promise per day. Visible evidence of follow-through. Let the pattern establish itself before life gets more complicated, before responsibilities multiply, before the margin for error shrinks.

Direct Loop 2 intentionally. Don't grow in whatever direction circumstances push you. Ask what capabilities you want to build. What skills will matter to you in ten years, not what skills are convenient to develop now.

This might mean saying no to growth opportunities that would build the wrong capabilities. It might mean seeking discomfort in areas that aren't immediately rewarded. It means treating your development as something you steer than something that happens to you.

The growth you do in this period compounds. Choose what compounds wisely.

Start feeding Loop 3 before it's urgent. You don't need to have your purpose figured out. You do need to be asking the question. What might matter beyond your own advancement? Where could contribution begin, even in small ways?

Start contributing now, even if the contribution is small. Start building the muscle of service before service becomes necessary. Start engaging the meaning question before the meaning question forces itself on you.

This doesn't mean derailing your career for volunteer work. It means noticing where your growing capabilities could benefit someone other than yourself. It means keeping the question alive rather than deferring it completely.

Set boundaries before you need them. The time to establish that you won't work weekends is before working weekends becomes the expectation. The time to protect recovery is before burnout makes it mandatory. The time to build patterns of regulation is while you still have the energy to sustain dysregulation.

Boundaries set early become defaults. Boundaries set late become struggles.

The patterns you establish now will be the patterns you inherit later. Choose them deliberately rather than letting circumstances choose them for you.

The opportunity.

The twenties and thirties are the highest-leverage period for loop work.

The patterns aren't yet fixed. The foundation can still be built than repaired. The growth can still be directed than redirected. The meaning question can still be engaged before crisis forces the engagement.

What you do in this period echoes. The foundation you build — or fail to build — is the foundation you'll stand on for the rest of your life. The capabilities you develop — or fail to develop — are the capabilities you'll have to work with. The relationship to meaning you establish — or fail to establish — shapes what the second half of life will feel like.

This isn't pressure. It's leverage. The work you do now has an outsized effect on everything that comes after.

Use the leverage. Build the foundation while building is easy. Direct the growth while you still have options. Engage the meaning question before it becomes a crisis.

The loops are forming. You get to influence how they form.

That's the opportunity of this stage. Don't waste it assuming there's always more time.

CHAPTER 14
LOOPS IN YOUR 40S AND 50S

"This is when the bills come due. What you deferred in your twenties becomes undeniable now."

This is when the bills come due.

The foundation you built — or didn't build — in your twenties and thirties now determines what's possible. The growth you directed — or let drift — now shows its trajectory. The meaning you engaged — or deferred — now demands an answer.

The forties and fifties are not a continuation of the earlier decades. They're a reckoning. The patterns that seemed to be working reveal their costs. The questions that could be postponed become impossible to ignore. The loops that were running in the background move to the foreground.

This is where midlife crisis comes from. Not from aging itself — from loop problems that were never addressed finally becoming undeniable.

What's being demanded.

Loop 2 is plateauing. The growth that defined your twenties and thirties is slowing down. Not stopping — but the returns are diminishing. You've built most of the capability you're going to build. The skills are established. The career has taken its shape. The body is no longer infinitely adaptable.

This isn't failure. It's natural. Growth can't accelerate forever. At some point, the curve flattens. The question becomes: what now? If your identity was fused with growth, this plateau feels like death. If growth was serving something larger, this plateau is a transition.

Loop 3 is demanding attention. The meaning question that could be deferred in your twenties can't be deferred anymore. You've built things. You've achieved things. Now what? Who does this matter to? What was it all for?

This question arrives whether you invite it or not. It arrives in the quiet moments. It arrives when the achievement that used to satisfy stops satisfying. It arrives when you look at what you've built and feel nothing.

If you've been feeding Loop 3 all along, this is a deepening. The contribution expands. The meaning matures. The question has an answer, even if the answer keeps evolving.

If you've been starving Loop 3, this is a crisis. The emptiness that was always there becomes impossible to ignore. The "why bother" question gets loud. The success that was supposed to mean something turns out to mean nothing.

Identity must mature. The identity that worked in your thirties won't work in your fifties. The achiever identity, the builder identity, the striver identity — these were appropriate for a growth phase. They become prisons in a plateau phase.

Mature identity isn't about what you produce. It's about who you are when you're not producing. It's about worth that doesn't depend on output. It's about knowing yourself beyond your achievements.

This transition is hard. It feels like loss. The identity that got you here has to partially die for the identity that will carry you forward to emerge.

. . .

What typically breaks.

The achiever hits the wall. You optimized for Loop 2 for twenty years. You built the career, accumulated the wins, became someone who produces. And now the growth is slowing, and you don't know who you are without the acceleration.

The wall isn't external. It's internal. The engine that was running is still running, but there's nowhere left to go. You've climbed the ladder and discovered it was leaning against the wrong wall — or that there's nothing at the top worth having.

This produces frantic activity. Doubling down on achievement. Chasing bigger targets to recreate the feeling of growth. Starting over in a new field to get back on the steep part of the curve. None of it works, because the problem isn't insufficient growth. The problem is that growth was never connected to meaning.

The deferred meaning question explodes. You told yourself you'd figure out purpose later. Later is now. And you don't have an answer.

This produces the classic midlife crisis symptoms. The sudden questioning of everything. The impulse to blow up your life. The desperate search for something — anything — that feels meaningful. The affair, the sports car, the radical career change. These are attempts to manufacture meaning through novelty when meaning was never built through contribution.

The foundation cracks show. If Loop 1 was never properly built, the cracks become visible now. The self-trust issues that were manageable in your thirties — when you had energy to compensate — become unmanageable in your forties. The pattern of broken promises, the chronic negotiation with yourself, the gap between knowing and doing — it's all still there. And you're more tired now.

The cracked foundation also undermines everything else. You can't address the meaning question if you can't trust yourself to follow through. You can't navigate the growth plateau if you're still fighting yourself on basic commitments. The foundation problems cascade upward.

Relationships strain. The loop patterns you've been running affect the people around you. The partner who tolerated your workaholism for twenty years runs out of patience. The children you were going to connect with "when things slow down" are now teenagers who don't know you. The friendships you neglected have atrophied.

The relational cost of loop dysfunction often comes due in this decade. You looked up from the achievement and discovered you're alone — or alone in a house full of people who've stopped expecting anything from you.

The common mistakes.
Mistake 1: Doubling down on Loop 2.
The growth is slowing, so you push harder. Work more. Achieve more. Start a new company, chase a new title, prove you're still in the game.

This is using the wrong loop for the problem. The problem isn't insufficient growth. The problem is that growth without meaning has run its course. More growth won't fix it. It will exhaust you while the actual problem remains unaddressed.

Mistake 2: Abandoning everything.
The opposite mistake. The meaning question arrives, and you conclude that everything you built was wrong. Quit the job. Leave the marriage. Move to a new city. Start over completely.

Sometimes this is necessary. Often it's avoidance. You're not addressing the meaning question — you're running from the life where the question became undeniable. The question will follow you. It doesn't care about your geography.

Mistake 3: Numbing the question.
The meaning question is uncomfortable. So you numb it.

Alcohol, work, affairs, screens, busyness — anything to avoid sitting with the emptiness.

This works temporarily. The question is patient. It will wait. And while it waits, you're wasting years you could be using to address it.

Mistake 4: Blaming external circumstances.

The job is the problem. The marriage is the problem. The industry, the economy, the culture — something out there is why you feel empty.

External circumstances might be part of it. But the loop problems are internal. You could change every external circumstance and still feel empty if the meaning loop is starved and the foundation is cracked. The work is internal. Blaming externals is avoidance.

What helps.

Accept the plateau. Growth is slowing. That's not failure — it's a phase transition. The task isn't to fight the plateau. It's to shift what you're optimizing for.

This requires grieving. The achiever identity has to partially die. The sense of yourself as someone on an upward trajectory has to evolve. This is loss. It's appropriate to feel it as loss.

But on the other side of that grief is freedom. You don't have to keep proving yourself. You don't have to keep climbing. You can start asking what all the climbing was for — and directing what you've built toward something that matters.

The plateau isn't the end. It's a vantage point. You can see further from here than you could while climbing.

Address the meaning question directly. Don't numb it. Don't run from it. Don't wait for it to resolve itself.

Ask: What would make this effort worthwhile? Who could benefit from what I've built? What contribution is possible now that wasn't possible before?

Start contributing. Not dramatically — start. Find somewhere your accumulated capability could serve something beyond yourself. Build the meaning loop you neglected to build earlier. It's not too late. It's more urgent.

The meaning question doesn't go away by being ignored. It gets louder. Better to engage it now than to let it corrode everything while you pretend it isn't there.

Repair the foundation if it's cracked. If Loop 1 is broken, this is the time to fix it. Not because it's convenient — it's not. Because everything else depends on it.

The same protocol applies: small promises, kept consistently, visible evidence. It's harder now because you have less energy and more demands. But it's also more necessary, because you can't navigate the meaning question or the growth plateau without a foundation to stand on.

If you've been compensating for a broken foundation with willpower and energy for twenty years, you're running out of both. The compensation stops working. The foundation has to be repaired.

Renegotiate relationships. The loop patterns you've been running have affected the people around you. If you're changing those patterns, the relationships need to change too.

This means honest conversation. Acknowledging what your patterns cost. Making amends where amends are possible. And accepting that some relationships may not survive the transition — either because they were built on dysfunction, or because too much damage has accumulated.

The relationships that can flex will deepen. The relationships that can't will strain. Both outcomes are information about what was real and what was accommodation.

Build an identity beyond achievement. Who are you when you're not producing? What matters to you beyond output? What would remain if the career disappeared tomorrow?

These questions are uncomfortable for people whose identity fused with achievement. They're also necessary. The identity that got you here won't carry you through the next phase. Something has to evolve.

This isn't about abandoning achievement. It's about not needing achievement to know who you are. About having a self that exists when the producing stops. About maturity.

The opportunity.

The forties and fifties are not decline. They're transition.

The growth phase is ending. The meaning phase is beginning. The identity that served the first half of life is giving way to the identity that will serve the second half.

This transition can be a crisis. Or it can be a reconfiguration.

The difference is whether you address the loops directly. Whether you accept what's changing instead of fighting it. Whether you do the work that the phase requires instead of the work that worked before.

The meaning that was optional in your twenties is essential now. The foundation that could be compensated for is now determinative. The identity that could be deferred must now be faced.

This is the reckoning. Not punishment — reckoning. An accounting of what was built and what was neglected. A chance to address what needs addressing before the next phase begins.

The loops are still running. The question is whether you'll run them consciously — or let them run you into the ground while you pretend nothing has changed.

Something has changed. The task is to change with it.

Common mistakes (40s and 50s):

- **Doubling down on what worked before.** The growth strategy that built your career isn't the strategy that will navigate this phase. More effort in the same direction produces diminishing returns. The phase demands something different. Recognize it.

- **Treating the meaning question as a crisis to be solved quickly.** You've deferred this question for twenty years. It doesn't get answered in a weekend. The impulse to blow everything up and start over is usually avoidance wearing the mask of boldness. Sit with the discomfort. The answer emerges through engagement, not escape.
- **Blaming external circumstances for internal problems.** The job, the marriage, the industry—something external is why you feel empty. Sometimes that's true. Often it's misdirection. The loop problems are internal. Changing geography won't fix structural dysfunction.
- **Resisting the plateau.** Growth is slowing. Fighting this fact exhausts you without changing it. The plateau isn't failure. It's a phase transition. Accept it, and you can use it. Resist it, and you waste years fighting reality.
- **Ignoring relational damage.** Twenty years of loop dysfunction left marks on the people around you. Pretending otherwise won't repair them. Some damage can be addressed. Some can't. Either way, denial makes it worse.

CHAPTER 15
LOOPS AT 60 AND BEYOND

"The question is no longer what you can build. It's what you can pass on."

This is the phase no one prepares you for.

The twenties and thirties were about building. The forties and fifties were about reckoning. The sixties and beyond are about something else entirely: transmission.

The question is no longer what you can build. It's what you can pass on. The focus shifts from accumulation to contribution, from proving to offering, from climbing to sharing the view.

This transition doesn't happen automatically. Many people enter this phase still running the loops of earlier decades — still chasing growth that's no longer available, still avoiding meaning questions that have become urgent, still trying to prove something to people who stopped watching long ago.

The loops don't retire when you do. They keep running. The question is whether you'll run them appropriately for this stage — or exhaust yourself fighting a phase transition that's already happened.

. . .

What's being demanded.

Loop 3 becomes primary. This is the meaning phase. Not meaning as an addition to achievement — meaning as the main event. The question of what your life was for moves from background to foreground. The answer either exists or it doesn't.

If you've been building Loop 3 throughout your life, this transition is natural. The contribution deepens. The service continues. The meaning that was always there becomes more central, more refined, more essential.

If you've been starving Loop 3, this transition is brutal. You arrive at the phase where meaning should be primary, and there's nothing there. The emptiness that could be outrun at forty can't be outrun at sixty-five. The question that could be numbed now demands an answer you don't have.

Loop 2 shifts from growth to maintenance. Growth doesn't stop, but it changes character. You're no longer building capability from scratch. You're maintaining what you have, adapting to new limitations, preserving function than expanding it.

This requires a different relationship with the body, with work, with challenge. The edges you push against are different now — not the edges of maximum performance, but the edges of continued function. The goal isn't to be stronger than you were. It's to remain capable of what matters.

Loop 1 faces its final test. Self-trust in this phase isn't about productivity promises. It's about deeper commitments. Can you trust yourself to face decline honestly? To adapt to limitation without collapse? To remain who you are as capacity diminishes?

The foundation you built — or failed to build — now supports everything else. If it's solid, you can navigate this phase with dignity. If it's cracked, the cracks become chasms.

Transmission, not accumulation.

The central task of this phase is transmission. Passing on

what you've learned. Offering what you've built. Contributing not through new creation but through sharing what's already been created.

This is different from earlier contribution. In your forties, contribution might have been about building something that serves others. In your sixties and beyond, contribution is increasingly about transfer — knowledge to younger people, resources to causes that will outlast you, wisdom to those who can still use it.

Accumulation becomes irrelevant. You can't take it with you. The question isn't how much you can gather but how much you can give away. The measure isn't what you have but what you've enabled.

This shift is hard for people who spent decades in accumulation mode. The habits of gathering, protecting, growing the pile — these don't serve anymore. They become obstacles to the task at hand.

Transmission requires letting go. Letting go of control over what you've built. Letting go of the need to be central. Letting go of the identity that was tied to accumulation. Holding loosely what you once held tightly, so it can pass to hands that will carry it forward.

What typically breaks.

Resistance to the phase itself. The most common failure is refusing to accept that this phase has arrived. Still trying to compete with younger people. Still measuring yourself by the metrics of earlier decades. Still treating growth as the primary goal when transmission should be.

This resistance is exhausting. You're fighting against time, against biology, against the natural arc of a human life. You can't win. And the fighting consumes energy that could be directed toward what this phase offers.

Bitterness about what wasn't built. If Loop 3 was starved, if meaning was deferred until there's no more time to build it, bitterness often follows. Resentment toward others who seem to have found purpose. Cynicism about meaning itself. The conclusion that it was all pointless — not because it was, but because you never connected your effort to anything that would make it otherwise.

Bitterness is the tax on deferred meaning. The longer you wait, the higher the tax.

Isolation through irrelevance. The person who was defined by their role — their job, their position, their function — loses that definition in this phase. The title is gone. The office is gone. The daily proof of relevance is gone. Without something else to replace it, isolation follows.

This isn't loneliness. It's the experience of not mattering. Of being surplus. Of occupying space without contributing to anything. The loop that should be running — contribution, service, transmission — isn't running because it was never built.

Denial of limitation. The body changes. Capacity diminishes. This is reality, not failure. But people who never learned to adapt, who powered through every obstacle, who treated limitation as something to overcome — they often can't accept what's happening.

Denial doesn't change the facts. It prevents adaptation. The person in denial makes choices based on who they used to be than who they are. They take risks their body can't support. They make promises their capacity can't keep. The gap between self-image and reality widens until something breaks.

The common mistakes.

Mistake 1: Trying to stay in the game.

The game has changed. The metrics that mattered at forty don't matter at sixty-five. The competition you were in has moved on. Trying to stay in it — still proving, still climbing, still achieving — is running Loop 2 when Loop 3 should be primary.

This isn't about giving up ambition. It's about redirecting it. The ambition to build can become the ambition to transmit. The drive to achieve can become the drive to enable others' achievement. The energy is still there. The direction needs to shift.

Mistake 2: Withdrawal instead of transmission.

Some people respond to this phase by retreating. They've done their part. Now they're done. They withdraw from contribution, from connection, from engagement with the world.

This is Loop 3 avoidance wearing retirement clothes. The need to contribute doesn't end because you've stopped working. The meaning question doesn't disappear because you've left the career behind. Withdrawal isn't peace — it's stagnation. And stagnation in this phase accelerates decline.

Mistake 3: Transmission without release.

Some people want to pass things on but can't let go. They mentor but control. They give but with strings attached. They offer wisdom but require that it be followed exactly.

This isn't transmission. It's extended accumulation. True transmission means releasing control over what you pass on. The knowledge you share will be adapted. The resources you transfer will be used differently than you would use them. The people you mentor will make their own choices.

If you can't release, you're not transmitting. You're hoarding with extra steps.

Mistake 4: Ignoring the foundation.

Even in this phase, Loop 1 matters. The commitments you make to yourself — to health, to relationships, to continued engagement — still need to be kept. The foundation doesn't become irrelevant because the structure built on it is changing.

People who neglect Loop 1 in this phase decline faster than they need to. They stop keeping promises to themselves about movement, about connection, about staying engaged. The foundation crumbles, and everything else crumbles with it.

. . .

What helps.

Accept the phase. This is where you are. Not where you were. Not where you wish you were. Here. Acceptance isn't defeat — it's the prerequisite for functioning well within reality.

Acceptance means grieving what's ending. The strength you had. The role you played. The future that's now shorter than the past. This grief is appropriate. It's not weakness. It's the honest response to genuine loss.

On the other side of acceptance is presence. You're here now. This phase has its own demands and its own offerings. You can meet them — but only if you stop fighting the fact that this is where you are.

Transmit actively. Don't wait to be asked. Offer what you have. Share what you've learned. Find the people and causes that could benefit from what you've accumulated, and start the transfer.

This might be mentoring. It might be teaching. It might be philanthropy. It might be being present for people who need what you can offer. The form matters less than the function — directing what you have toward those who can use it.

Maintain the foundation. Keep promises to yourself. Small ones, daily. The practices that maintain function — movement, connection, engagement — need to continue. The foundation doesn't maintain itself.

This becomes harder as capacity diminishes. The promises might need to be smaller. The practices might need to adapt. But the principle remains: self-trust is built and maintained through kept commitments. That doesn't change because you're older.

Find contribution that matches current capacity. You can't contribute the way you did at forty. But you can contribute. The question is finding the form that matches what you can offer now.

This might be less intense than before. It might be different in kind. It might require accepting that your contribution is now one of presence than production. But it's still contribution. It still matters. It still feeds the meaning loop.

Prepare for the end without being consumed by it. Death is coming. That's not morbid — it's factual. This phase involves preparation for an end that's no longer abstract.

Preparing doesn't mean obsessing. It means getting affairs in order. Making peace where peace can be made. Saying what needs to be said. Ensuring that what you want to transmit gets transmitted.

People who avoid this preparation leave chaos behind. People who become consumed by it miss the life that's still here. The balance is preparation without preoccupation.

The opportunity.

This phase offers something the earlier phases don't: freedom from the need to become.

You are who you are. The building is done. The becoming has happened. Now you can be — and offer what you've become to those still building.

This is freedom. Not the freedom of youth, which is freedom to become anything. The freedom of age, which is freedom from having to become anything else. You're here. This is you. Now you can give it away.

Transmission is the culmination of the loops. Everything you built with Loop 2, everything you grounded with Loop 1, everything you connected to meaning with Loop 3 — it all becomes available for transfer. Not lost at the end. Passed on. Continued in different forms, in different people, in the ongoing stream of human life.

That's what this phase is for. Not diminishment. Transmission.

The loops keep running until they don't. The question is what you do with them while they're still yours to run.

• • •

Common mistakes (60+):

- **Refusing to accept the phase.** You're still trying to compete with younger people. Still measuring yourself by metrics that no longer apply. Still treating transmission as surrender rather than as this phase's actual work. The resistance is exhausting. The phase has arrived whether you accept it or not.
- **Withdrawing instead of transmitting.** You've done your part. Now you're done. This feels like rest but functions as stagnation. The loop that should be running—contribution, transmission, passing on what you've built—isn't running. Withdrawal accelerates decline.
- **Transmitting with strings attached.** You'll share what you know, but only if it's implemented exactly as you would do it. This isn't transmission. It's extended control. True transmission requires letting go. What you pass on will be adapted, changed, used in ways you wouldn't use it. That's appropriate.
- **Treating limitation as failure.** The body changes. Capacity diminishes. This is reality, not personal defeat. Denial doesn't change the facts. It just prevents adaptation. The people who age well adapt to limitation without collapsing into it.[1]
- **Deferring transmission until "the right time."** The right time is now. Later might not come. The knowledge you carry, the resources you've built, the wisdom you've earned—these don't get more transmissible by waiting. They get lost.

PART SEVEN
BOUNDARIES

CHAPTER 16
WHEN THIS BOOK ISN'T ENOUGH

"This book has limits. Some problems require different tools. Knowing which is which—that's diagnostic clarity."

This book has limits.

Everything covered so far — the three loops, their failure modes, the repair protocols, the life-stage transitions — applies to a specific range of human dysfunction. The range is wide. It covers most of what people experience as stuckness, burnout, emptiness, and chronic self-defeat.

But it doesn't cover everything.

Some conditions look like loop problems but aren't. Some situations require intervention this book cannot provide. Some people need help that no framework, no matter how accurate, can deliver through pages alone.

Knowing when you've exceeded the book's scope isn't weakness. It's the same diagnostic clarity that makes everything else work. You have to know which tool fits the problem. And sometimes the right tool isn't a book.

The distinction that matters.

Loop problems are structural. They involve feedback systems running incorrectly — wrong sequence, wrong emphasis, broken mechanics.[1] The person with loop problems has a functioning system that's misconfigured. The repair is reconfiguration: correct the sequence, rebuild the foundation, regulate what's dysregulated.

Pathology is different. Pathology involves damage that structural reconfiguration cannot address. The system isn't misconfigured — parts of it are injured, compromised, or operating outside normal parameters. Reconfiguration doesn't help when the components themselves need repair that's beyond self-directed work.

This distinction isn't always clean. Loop problems and pathology can coexist. Trauma can cause loop problems, and loop problems can worsen trauma responses. Depression can look like meaning starvation, and meaning starvation can trigger depression. The categories blur at the edges.

But the distinction still matters. Because the interventions are different. And applying the wrong intervention — treating pathology as a loop problem, or treating a loop problem as pathology — makes things worse.

What this book cannot address.

Trauma that lives in the body.

Some people carry trauma that hasn't been processed. Not difficult memories — physiological patterns encoded in the nervous system. Hyper vigilance. Dissociation. Triggered responses that bypass conscious control. The body remembers what the mind has tried to forget.

Loop repair assumes a nervous system that can update based on new evidence. Trauma often prevents that update. The system is stuck in a protective mode that made sense during the original threat but no longer serves the current environment.

New evidence doesn't land because the body isn't receiving it — it's still responding to something that happened years ago.

This requires more than kept promises and deliberate discomfort. It requires therapeutic work that specifically addresses trauma — approaches that work with the body, not the mind. EMDR, somatic experiencing, trauma-focused therapy. Interventions designed to help the nervous system complete responses that got frozen.

If you recognize yourself here — if your reactions seem disproportionate to current circumstances, if certain triggers send you into states you can't control, if your body carries tension that never releases despite your best efforts — the loop model isn't wrong for you. It's incomplete. You need something this book cannot provide.

When symptoms overlap: Differential diagnosis

Some experiences signal multiple possible loop failures. Exhaustion, for example, can mean three different things.

If you're exhausted and:

- You can't keep promises to yourself + You negotiate every commitment + Motivation vanishes before action begins = *Loop 1 is broken*

If you're exhausted and:

- You can't stop working + Rest feels like failure + You're productive but hollowing out = *Loop 2 is dysregulated*

If you're exhausted and:

- Success feels empty + You can't answer "why bother?" + Achievement doesn't satisfy = *Loop 3 is starved*

· · ·

If you're stuck and:
- You know what to do but can't do it + Insight doesn't change behavior + Self-talk is sophisticated but action is absent = *Loop 1 is broken*

If you're stuck and:
- Everything is comfortable + Challenge is systematically avoided + Growth has stopped but you've rationalized why = *Loop 2 is being avoided*

If you're stuck and:
- Achievement is high but satisfaction is low + You're climbing ladders against the wrong walls + Wins don't land = *Loop 3 is starved*

The diagnostic question isn't just "what hurts?" It's "what pattern produces this specific hurt?" Different patterns require different repairs.

Addiction that has taken hold.

Addiction hijacks the loop system. It creates artificial feedback that overrides natural signals. The substance or behavior produces reward that nothing else can match, and the system reorganizes around pursuing that reward.

This looks like a Loop 1 problem — broken promises, chronic negotiation, the gap between knowing and doing. And in early stages, it might respond to Loop 1 repair. But once addiction has established itself neurologically, willpower and small promises aren't enough. The reward circuitry has been altered. The system is no longer misconfigured — it's been chemically restructured.

Addiction recovery requires specific intervention. Medical

support for physical dependence. Therapeutic frameworks designed for addictive patterns. Often community structures that provide external support when internal systems can't be trusted. The loop model can complement recovery, but it cannot replace the specialized help addiction requires.

If you're managing a substance or behavior that has become compulsive — if you've tried to stop repeatedly and can't, if the cost is obvious and you still continue, if the addiction has begun organizing your life around it — you need more than this book. You need intervention designed for what addiction is.

Mental health conditions that require clinical treatment.

Depression is not the same as meaning starvation, though they can feel similar. Anxiety disorders are not the same as broken self-trust, though they produce overlapping symptoms. Bipolar disorder, schizophrenia, severe OCD, personality disorders — these are clinical conditions that require clinical treatment.

The loop model describes normal human functioning and its common malfunctions. Mental health conditions often involve abnormal functioning — neurochemistry that's dysregulated, perceptual systems that distort reality, emotional responses that operate outside typical ranges.

Some of these conditions can be managed with the right treatment. Medication, specialized therapy, ongoing clinical support. But they cannot be managed with self-directed structural work alone. The attempt to treat a clinical condition as a loop problem delays appropriate care and can make the condition worse.

If you suspect — or know — that you have a mental health condition, get professional evaluation. The loop model might be useful alongside treatment. It cannot substitute for it.

Suicidal ideation or active self-harm.

This needs to be stated directly. If you're having thoughts of ending your life, if you're harming yourself, if you're in crisis —

this book is not the appropriate resource. You need immediate support.

Crisis lines exist for this reason. Mental health professionals can provide emergency intervention. Hospitals have psychiatric services for acute situations.

The loop model assumes someone who is working on optimization within a functioning life. Someone in crisis needs stabilization first. Get help. The loops will still be here when you're stable enough to work on them.

Signals that you've exceeded the book's scope.

How do you know when loop work isn't enough? The line isn't always obvious. Here are signals that suggest you need more than self-directed structural repair.

The symptoms are too severe. Loop problems produce discomfort — chronic negotiation, exhaustion, hollowness. But they don't typically produce incapacitation. If you can't get out of bed, can't take care of basic needs, can't function at even minimal levels — something beyond loop dysfunction is happening.

The patterns don't respond to intervention. You've tried the protocols. You've kept the small promises. You've engaged the discomfort. And nothing shifts. After weeks of consistent effort, the experience is identical to before you started.

Specifically: If you've applied the Loop 1 repair protocol—small promises, kept consistently, visible evidence—for eight weeks with zero subjective progress, that's a signal. Not moral failure. Diagnostic information.

Eight weeks is enough time for the self-trust loop to begin updating if it's going to update through this approach. If it hasn't, one of three things is true:

1. The diagnosis was wrong (it's not actually a Loop 1 problem)

2. The application was incorrect (promises too large, evidence not visible, consistency not genuine)
3. The problem exceeds self-directed structural repair (trauma, addiction, clinical condition)

The appropriate response isn't to try harder with the same protocol. It's to seek professional assessment. A therapist or psychiatrist can evaluate what this book cannot.

The same principle applies to Loop 2 and Loop 3 work. If you've genuinely applied the repair protocols for two months with no shift—if the experience is identical, if the patterns are unchanged, if nothing has moved—that's information. The book has limits. You've reached them. That's not failure. That's knowing when to use a different tool.

Some resistance is normal. Loops don't repair instantly. But complete non-response is a signal. Either the diagnosis is wrong (it's not a loop problem), or something else is blocking the repair (trauma, neurochemistry, conditions that require different intervention).

The origin is identifiable and traumatic. If you can trace your current dysfunction to specific traumatic events — abuse, violence, severe loss, life-threatening experiences — the dysfunction might be trauma response than loop misconfiguration. The events left marks that loop work alone won't address.

The experience includes symptoms beyond the loop model. Hallucinations. Delusions. Dissociative episodes. Manic phases. Panic attacks that feel life-threatening. Compulsions that override all other considerations.

The loop model describes feedback systems. It doesn't describe psychosis, dissociation, mania, or panic disorder. If your experience includes these phenomena, you need evaluation and treatment designed for what you're experiencing.

You've been told by professionals. If a therapist, psychiatrist, or physician has diagnosed you with a condition and recommended treatment, that recommendation exists for a reason. The loop model is not a substitute for professional medical or psychological care.

The situation involves danger. Danger to yourself or others. Situations where the stakes have moved beyond optimization into genuine risk. Loop work assumes a safe container. If the container isn't safe, safety comes first.

How to seek help without shame.

Many people resist professional help. The resistance has many sources — cost, access, stigma, past bad experiences, the belief that they should be able to handle it themselves.

Some of these barriers are real. Professional help costs money. Good providers aren't always available. Past experiences with therapy or psychiatry might have been unhelpful or even harmful.

But the resistance is often also loop-related. Broken Loop 1 makes it hard to follow through on seeking help. Dysregulated Loop 2 frames needing help as failure. Starved Loop 3 produces cynicism about whether anything can help.

Seeking help is not a loop failure. It's loop intelligence. Knowing which problems exceed your tools and finding appropriate resources — that's diagnostic accuracy, not weakness.

Here's what seeking help requires.

Acknowledge the limit honestly. Not as self-criticism. As assessment. "This exceeds what I can address on my own" is information, not judgment. The same clarity that diagnoses a loop problem can diagnose when professional help is needed.

Start with evaluation. You don't have to commit to long-term treatment to get assessed. A single appointment with a therapist or psychiatrist can provide diagnostic clarity. You might discover you have a condition that explains your experience. You might discover you don't. Either way, you'll have better information.

Match the provider to the problem. Not all therapists are the same. Not all approaches work for all conditions. Someone specializing in trauma will be more useful for trauma than a generalist. Someone experienced with addiction will be more useful for addiction than someone who isn't.

Do some research. Ask what approaches they use. Ask about their experience with your specific situation. A provider who isn't a good fit isn't better than no provider — but a good fit can change everything.

Give it time. Professional treatment often takes time to work. Therapy requires building a relationship and working through material. Medication requires finding the right type and dosage. The first provider might not be the right one.

The same patience that loop repair requires applies to professional treatment. Expecting immediate transformation sets up disappointment. Expect gradual progress, with adjustments along the way.

Use the loop model alongside treatment. Professional help doesn't mean abandoning everything in this book. The loops still exist. Self-trust still matters. Growth still needs regulation. Meaning still requires building.

The loop model can complement professional treatment. It provides a structural framework for the work you're doing. It gives language to patterns you might be exploring in therapy. It offers practices that support clinical interventions.

The combination often works better than either alone. Professional help addresses what professionals are equipped to address. Loop work addresses what structural repair can address. Together they cover more ground.

What professional help provides that this book cannot.

Objective assessment. A professional sees you from outside. They can identify patterns you can't see, ask questions you wouldn't think to ask, notice things your self-observation misses. The external perspective is itself therapeutic.

Specialized training. Therapists and psychiatrists have

training in conditions and interventions this book doesn't cover. They know approaches you don't know. They've seen patterns in other people that illuminate your situation.

Accountability and structure. Regular appointments create external structure. Someone is tracking your progress. Someone is expecting you to show up. For people whose Loop 1 is badly broken, this external accountability can bridge the gap until internal accountability rebuilds.

Safe space for processing. Some things are hard to process alone. Trauma, grief, shame — they often require a witness. Someone who can receive what you're carrying without being damaged by it. That's what good therapeutic relationships provide.

Medical intervention when needed. Some conditions have biological components that respond to medication. Depression can be neurochemical. Anxiety can be neurochemical. These conditions don't mean you're weak — they mean your brain chemistry needs support that talk and structure alone can't provide.

Crisis intervention. If things get acute, professionals have resources for stabilization that you don't have access to alone. Hospitalization when needed. Crisis intervention. Safety planning. The infrastructure that catches you when self-directed work isn't enough.

The goal is functioning, not purity.

Some people resist professional help because it feels like failure. Like they should be able to handle everything themselves. Like needing help means the framework doesn't work or they're not trying hard enough.

This is Loop 2 dysfunction dressed as self-reliance. The drive to handle everything through personal effort, extended into a domain where personal effort isn't sufficient.

The goal isn't to fix yourself without help. The goal is to function. To have a life that works. To resolve the suffering that can be resolved and manage what can be managed.

If that requires professional help, professional help is the right tool. Using the right tool isn't failure. It's competence.

The loops will still be here. The foundation still needs building. Growth still needs regulating. Meaning still requires earning. But if those projects are blocked by conditions that require clinical intervention, getting that intervention is the first step.

Not instead of the loops. Before them. Or alongside them.

A final note on boundaries.

This chapter exists because the book needed to say it clearly: there are limits to what structural work can accomplish.

Some readers will recognize themselves in what's been described. They'll realize they've been trying to loop-repair their way through something that requires different intervention. For them, this chapter is permission — permission to seek help without it meaning the framework is wrong or they are.

Other readers will read this chapter and confirm that their situation falls within the book's scope. Their problems are loop problems. The structural repairs apply. They can proceed with the protocols knowing they're using the right tool for their situation.

Either outcome is useful. Clarity about what you're dealing with is always useful.

The loops run your life. Understanding them gives you leverage over problems you couldn't see before. But understanding has limits. Some problems require more than understanding, more than self-directed work, more than any book can provide.

Knowing which is which — that's the diagnostic skill this entire book has been building toward. It applies here too.

Know your limits. Know the book's limits. Seek appropriate help when help is needed.

Then continue with what remains.

The loops will still be there. The work will still be there. Whatever condition you're addressing, whatever professional help you're receiving, the structural questions remain:

Do you trust your own word?

Are you growing where growth is needed?

Does your effort connect to something that matters?

These questions don't disappear because you have a diagnosis. They become clearer. The noise of unaddressed conditions gets removed. What's left is the structural work that the loops describe.

Handle what needs handling. Then build what can be built.

That's the path forward, regardless of where you're starting from.

PART EIGHT
CLOSING

CHAPTER 17
A COHERENT HUMAN LIFE

"Coherence isn't calm. It's effort going where effort should go."

This is what it looks like when the loops run well.

Not perfectly. Not optimally. Not in some idealized state that exists only in books and fantasies. Well. Functioning as they should, in the right sequence, serving what they're meant to serve.

A coherent life isn't calm. It isn't easy. It isn't the absence of difficulty or the presence of constant satisfaction. Coherence is something else entirely: the experience of effort going where effort should go. Of action matching intention. Of a life that makes sense to the person living it.

Most people never experience this. Not because they're incapable, but because they've never seen the machinery clearly enough to run it properly. They push when they should stabilize. They serve when they should grow. They chase meaning while their foundation crumbles. The effort is real. The direction is wrong.

Coherence is what happens when the direction is right.

. . .

What coherence is not.

It's not balance. Balance implies equal distribution — the same attention to each loop, the same energy in each direction. That's not how it works. Different seasons demand different loops. Different problems require different responses. The person trying to maintain perfect balance is the person who never gives anything the attention it needs.

It's not optimization. Optimization implies a maximum — some theoretical peak state where everything runs at full capacity forever. That state doesn't exist. The pursuit of it produces the dysfunction the loops are meant to prevent. Coherence isn't about maximizing. It's about fitting.

It's not peace. Peace implies the absence of tension, and tension is part of being alive. Growth requires tension. Contribution creates tension. Even self-trust involves the tension between what you want to do and what you said you would do. Coherence doesn't eliminate tension. It makes tension productive.

It's not arrival. There's no point where you've made it, where the work is done, where you can stop attending to the loops because they've been perfected. The loops keep running until you die. The work is ongoing. Coherence isn't a destination. It's a way of traveling.

What coherence looks like.

Your word means something.

When you say you'll do something, you do it. Not always — no one keeps every promise. But consistently enough that you believe yourself. Consistently enough that your system invests in your intentions than dismissing them.

This doesn't look dramatic from the outside. It looks like someone who shows up. Who follows through. Who doesn't need external accountability for every commitment because internal accountability is functioning.

The alarm goes off, and you get up. Not because you feel like it — because that's what you said you would do. The project needs work, and you work on it. Not because motivation struck — because you committed. The boundary needs holding, and you hold it. Not because it's easy — because your word is worth keeping.

This is Loop 1 running cleanly. The foundation is solid. Everything else has something to stand on.

Growth serves rather than consumes.

You push yourself — but not past the point of extraction. You seek challenge — but you also recover. You build capability — but capability isn't all you are.

The person with regulated growth can work hard and then stop. Can achieve without needing achievement to feel worthy. Can rest without guilt, be unproductive without shame, exist without constantly optimizing.

This doesn't mean they've stopped growing. It means growth has its place. It's a tool, not an identity. It serves the life rather than consuming it.

They know when to push and when to ease off. When the edge is productive and when it's self-punishment. When growth is building something and when it's running from something. The loop is bounded. The boundaries hold.

Effort connects to something that matters.

The work has direction. Not vague direction — felt direction. The person knows why they're doing what they're doing. The answer isn't "because I should" or "because others expect it" or "because I don't know what else to do." The answer connects to something beyond immediate personal gain.

This doesn't require grand purpose. It doesn't require saving the world or changing history. It requires contribution — some way that capability serves something other than its own accumulation.

Maybe it's raising children with presence. Maybe it's building something that helps people. Maybe it's mentoring, or creating, or showing up for others in ways that matter. The form varies. The function is the same: effort that connects to something larger than the self.

This produces a particular experience. The experience of mattering. Not in an inflated, narcissistic way — in a grounded way. The quiet knowledge that what you do makes a difference to something or someone. That the effort isn't motion.

A day in a coherent life.

The morning starts without negotiation. Not because every morning is easy — some aren't. But the basic commitments don't require debate. The alarm means get up. The practice means practice. The promises made yesterday are kept today.

There's work — and the work has purpose. Not every task is meaningful in isolation, but the work as a whole connects to something. The person knows why they're doing it. The effort doesn't feel arbitrary.

There's challenge. Something that requires stretching, learning, pushing against current limits. Not constant challenge — that's dysregulation. But regular enough that capability keeps building, that stagnation doesn't set in, that the growth loop turns.

There's recovery. Actual rest, not distraction. Time when the system rebuilds rather than extracts. This doesn't feel like failure. It feels like part of the rhythm.

There's connection. Some way that the day's effort touches others. Contribution, service, presence. Not constant giving — that's depletion. But enough that the meaning loop has something to work with.

The day ends with the sense that it was spent, not wasted. Not that every hour was productive — some weren't. But that the overall direction was right. That the effort went where it should have gone.

And tomorrow, the same. Not identical — conditions change. But the same basic coherence. Foundation holding. Growth serving. Meaning present.

This is what it looks like. Ordinary. Unremarkable from the outside. Profoundly different from the inside.

What this looks like in practice

Three lives. Three different phases. Three ways the loops run coherently.

Maya, 35, rebuilding self-trust

6:00am — Alarm. She gets up. No negotiation. This is the first kept promise of the day.

6:15am — Glass of water, make the bed. Two more promises kept. She notes them mentally but doesn't celebrate. Just registers: done.

6:30am — Twenty minutes of movement. Not a workout—just movement. Walking, stretching, something that reminds her body it exists. She doesn't feel like it most days. She does it anyway.

7:00am — Breakfast, then work begins. She's a designer. The work requires focus. She gives it focus—not because she's motivated, but because that's what she said she'd do.

12:30pm — Lunch break. She takes it. Actually stops. This was hard at first—Loop 2 kept wanting to push through. Now the boundary holds. Thirty minutes. Then back.

3:00pm — Afternoon slump. She takes a ten-minute walk instead of scrolling her phone. Another kept promise. The promise isn't "be productive every minute." It's "when you said you'd move, move."

6:00pm — Work ends. Laptop closes. The boundary is firm. There's always more work. There's always tomorrow.

6:30pm — Dinner, then presence. She lives alone, so presence means being here—not working, not planning, not optimizing. Just existing. Reading. Sketching. Sometimes nothing.

9:30pm — Phone on charger in the other room. Another promise. No scrolling in bed.

10:00pm — Lights out. Sleep comes or it doesn't. She's kept the promises she controls. That's enough.

What's not happening: Grand transformations. Peak performance. Optimized days.

What is happening: One kept promise after another. The gap between intention and action is closing. The self-trust loop is rebuilding. She can feel it. Not dramatically. Steadily.

David, 48, regulating growth

5:30am — Wakes naturally. No alarm. Sleep is no longer negotiable. Eight hours, non-negotiable.

6:00am — Movement, coffee, twenty minutes with nothing. Just sitting. This is new. Used to be: wake up, immediately working. Now: wake up, exist first, then work.

7:00am — Work begins. He's a founder. The company needs him. But it doesn't need him 16 hours a day. It needs him clear, rested, strategic. That requires boundaries.

9:00am — First meeting. He's present. Not checking messages. Not half-listening while planning the next thing. Present. When the meeting ends, it ends. He doesn't carry it into the next thing.

12:00pm — Lunch with his team. Not a working lunch. Lunch. They talk about life. They're humans, not resources. This took years to learn.

1:00pm — Deep work block. No meetings, no interruptions. Three hours of strategic work. This is where his actual value is. Not in being available constantly. In thinking clearly.

4:00pm — Work stops. Hard stop. Doesn't matter if something's unfinished. It will be there tomorrow. The world will not end because he stopped at 4pm.

4:30pm — Gym. Real workout. This is Loop 2 functioning properly—deliberate discomfort, skill building, capacity maintenance. But it's bounded. He's not training for a competition. He's maintaining the body that has to carry him for decades.

6:00pm — Home. Dinner with his wife. They talk. Really talk. Not about the company. About life. Their kids. Their plans. The relationship exists beyond his work. That's new.

8:00pm — Reading, sometimes a project he cares about but doesn't monetize. Painting. Writing. Something that exists for its own sake, not for output.

10:00pm — Bed. Eight hours. Non-negotiable.

What's not happening: Grinding. Proving. Using work to avoid himself.

What is happening: Bounded effort. Growth that serves life rather than consuming it. Achievement without identity fusion. He works hard. Then he stops. Both are possible.

Eleanor, 67, transmission mode

7:00am — Wakes slowly. No rushing. The urgency that drove her forties and fifties is gone. She's still capable. She's no longer frantic.

8:00am — Coffee, reading. She's catching up on her field—not to stay current for competition, but to know what's being built. She's interested. The pressure is gone.

9:00am — Emails. She mentors three younger professionals. They email questions. She responds—thoughtfully, without needing to control how they use the advice. She offers what she knows. They'll do what they'll do.

10:30am — Writing. She's documenting what she learned over 40 years in her field. Not for publication necessarily. For transmission. So it doesn't die with her. The writing is slow. That's appropriate. She's not racing anymore.

12:00pm — Lunch with a friend. Someone she's known for

decades. They talk about everything and nothing. The relationship exists for its own sake. There's no agenda.

1:30pm — Volunteer work. She teaches a workshop once a week at the community center. The participants are retirees learning new skills. She shares what she knows. Some of them get it. Some don't. She's okay with both. The contribution is the point, not the outcome.

3:30pm — Walk. Her knees aren't what they were. She walks anyway. Movement is still possible. She does what's possible.

5:00pm — Dinner prep. Cooking is meditative now. It used to be a chore squeezed between meetings. Now it's presence. She's here. The food is here. That's enough.

6:30pm — Evening. Sometimes she paints. Sometimes she just sits. Sometimes she calls her daughter. The days have space in them. She's not filling every hour. The space is intentional.

9:00pm — Bed. Sleep comes easier now than it did at 50. The striving is over. The transmission continues. That's coherence.

What's not happening: Accumulation. Proving. Building empire.

What is happening: Transmission. Presence. Contribution from fullness rather than deficit. She's passing on what she built. Not with desperation. With steadiness. The loops are running. Quietly. Coherently. That's what this phase looks like.

Three lives. Three phases. Same principle: the loops run in the right sequence, bounded appropriately, for the conditions at hand. Not perfect. Coherent. That's what it looks like when it works.

The texture of coherence.

There's a particular quality to life when the loops are running well.

Decisions become clearer. When you trust yourself, when growth is bounded, when meaning is present — decisions filter through that structure. You know what you're optimizing for.

You know what matters. The options that don't fit become obviously wrong. The options that do fit become obviously right.

This doesn't eliminate difficulty. Some decisions are genuinely hard. But the difficulty is in the situation, not in the self. You're not fighting yourself while also fighting the problem. You're addressing the problem.

Effort becomes sustainable. The white-knuckle pushing of dysregulated growth is gone. The paralysis of broken self-trust is gone. The emptiness of starved meaning is gone. What remains is effort that replenishes as it expends. Work that feeds rather than only extracts.

This doesn't mean energy is unlimited. It means energy goes where it should go. Less is wasted on internal friction. Less is lost to compensatory patterns. The effort that happens is the effort that matters.

Relationships become cleaner. When you're not using others to compensate for your broken loops, relationships simplify. You're not seeking validation because your self-trust is intact. You're not using others as fuel for achievement because growth is bounded. You're not martyring yourself because meaning is present without self-destruction.

What remains is connection. Actual connection. People relating to people, without the distortion of unaddressed loop dysfunction.

Identity becomes stable. Not rigid — stable. You know who you are. Not because you've figured everything out, but because the foundation holds. You're someone who keeps their word. You're someone who grows without being consumed. You're someone whose effort connects to something that matters.

This stability isn't fragile. It doesn't collapse when circumstances change. It doesn't require constant external validation. It's structural. Built from the inside.

What coherence requires.

It requires ongoing attention. The loops don't maintain themselves. The foundation can crack if neglected. Growth can dysregulate if unbounded. Meaning can starve if unfed. Coherence isn't achieved once and then preserved automatically. It's maintained through continued engagement.

This doesn't mean constant vigilance. It means periodic checking. Noticing when the signals appear. Responding when response is needed. The skill built throughout this book — reading which loop needs attention and providing it — that skill never becomes unnecessary. It becomes habitual.

It requires honesty. Honest assessment of which loop is broken, rather than which loop you'd prefer to work on. Honest acknowledgment of when professional help is needed, than insisting on self-repair past its limits. Honest recognition of when you're compensating, avoiding, or running the wrong loop for the problem you're in.

The loops don't respond to self-deception. They respond to reality. Honesty is the price of coherence.

It requires patience. The foundation takes time to rebuild. Growth regulation takes time to establish. Meaning takes time to earn. The person who wants coherence immediately gets none of it. The person who builds slowly, consistently, patiently — they get all of it.

Patience doesn't mean passivity. It means sustained action over time. The recognition that some things can't be rushed. That the loops update gradually. That the identity changes incrementally. That coherence is built in days and weeks and months, not in moments of insight or bursts of effort.

It requires acceptance. Acceptance that you're running these loops whether you like it or not. That the machinery exists and operates regardless of your philosophy about it. That the question isn't whether to engage the loops but how to engage them.

And acceptance that coherence isn't perfection. That you'll slip, misdiagnose, run the wrong loop sometimes. That the practice is ongoing and imperfect and human. That coherence

THE THREE LOOPS THAT RUN YOUR LIFE

includes the capacity to return when you've drifted — not the impossibility of ever drifting.

The alternative.

The alternative to coherence is what most people experience.

Effort that goes nowhere. Growth that consumes. Meaning that's either absent or premature. A foundation that's cracked and compensated for than repaired.

The alternative is knowing what to do and not doing it. Succeeding and feeling hollow. Helping others and falling apart. Pushing forever toward a satisfaction that never arrives.

The alternative is loop confusion. Running yesterday's loop in today's conditions. Using one loop to avoid another. Never quite understanding why nothing works despite all the effort.

Most people live this way. Not because they're broken. Because no one showed them the machinery. Because the loops are invisible until someone points them out. Because the culture offers solutions that don't match the problems.

You've now seen the machinery. You understand how the loops work. You know what breaks them and what repairs them. You know the sequence. You know the signals. You know when the book is enough and when it isn't.

The alternative — the confusion, the misdirection, the endless effort in the wrong direction — that alternative is no longer your only option.

The invitation.

This isn't a call to action. Not a motivational push. Not an inspirational finale that tries to send you out into the world with elevated feelings.

It's simpler than that.

The loops are running. They were running before you read this book. They'll keep running after you finish it. The machinery exists. The patterns operate. The feedback continues.

The only question is whether you'll engage the machinery consciously or let it run by default.

Default is what got most people where they are. Default is the compensation patterns, the confusion, the effort that never lands. Default is decades of running the wrong loop for the problem at hand.

Conscious engagement is different. It's seeing clearly which loop needs attention. It's providing that attention without over-complicating it. It's building foundation when foundation is needed. It's growing when growth is needed. It's serving when service is earned.

It's knowing when to push and when to stop. When to engage and when to rest. When the book is enough and when something else is required.

That's the invitation. Not to become a different person. To run the machinery you already have with clarity about what it needs.

A coherent human life isn't extraordinary.

From the outside, it looks ordinary. Someone who does what they say. Someone who works and rests. Someone who contributes without collapse. Someone who grows without being consumed. Someone who seems, somehow, to have their life working.

From the inside, it's the absence of the war. The war against yourself. The war between knowing and doing. The war between effort and emptiness. The war that most people fight every day without knowing there's an alternative.

Coherence is what happens when the war ends. Not through victory — through dissolution. The loops run properly. The conflict that was generated by their dysfunction disappears. What remains is life. Effort that makes sense. Rest that restores. Contribution that connects.

That's available. Not through insight alone — through structure. Through small promises kept. Through growth that serves. Through meaning that's earned.

The loops are already running. The machinery is already there.

Now you know what to do with it.

ABOUT THE AUTHOR

Lee Powell didn't set out to write a systems book. He set out to survive collapse.

On paper, his life worked: Oxford-educated, MSc. in engineering, founder of global software platforms. He built companies, sold companies, raised a family. By thirty, he had every measure of success — and still found himself empty, asking, *Is this it?*

The breakdown wasn't optional. It was lived. And it forced him into a rebuild that took years — years of figuring out which systems were broken and which efforts were pointed in the wrong direction. Out of that scar tissue came the framework in this book: not as theory, but as the operating logic he wished someone had shown him twenty years earlier.

Lee blends engineering precision with the human mess of recovery. His work resonates with people who know the grind: the years of building something from scratch, the exhaustion that doesn't resolve, the success that somehow doesn't satisfy. He knows what it looks like to have everything working on the outside while something fundamental is broken underneath.

He is also the author of *ManOS: Rebuild the Man Beneath the Mask*, which applies related principles to the specific challenges men face in rebuilding identity and integrity.

This book isn't a résumé line. It's a field report. If it helps you avoid even one of the crashes he lived through, then the scars weren't wasted.

For more of Lee's work, visit leepowell.com.

ALSO BY LEE POWELL

Lee Powell is a systems thinker, writer, and artist whose work focuses on how human lives function under pressure.

He is the author of *ManOS: Rebuild the Man Beneath the Mask*, a practical operating system for men navigating fracture, burnout, and identity collapse. *The Three Loops That Run Your Life* extends that work beyond gender, offering a clear, non-pathologizing model for how effort, growth, and meaning interact — and why so many capable people stall or exhaust themselves despite insight and discipline.

Lee's work rejects motivation, ideology, and emotional performance in favor of structure, sequence, and lived consequence. His writing is informed by direct experience of system failure — personal, relational, and professional — and by years spent building, breaking, and rebuilding complex systems where coherence mattered more than appearance.

Alongside his writing, Lee maintains an active art practice. One original painting accompanies each of the three loops in this book. The works are not illustrations of ideas, but parallel inquiries — visual explorations of fracture, alignment, pressure, and coherence that cannot be reduced to language alone.

The art and the writing come from the same place: an insistence on truth that holds up under real conditions.

Lee lives and works in Australia.

Learn more about his writing and artwork at: **leepowell.com**

For readers who want to apply the work of *ManOS* in a structured, real-world container, information about the ManOS system and cohorts can be found at: **getmanos.com**

INDEX

A

abandoned, 50, 56, 83, 104, 113, 118, 145, 201
abandonment, 26, 46, 90–91, 93, 97, 129, 201
accountability, 83, 108–109, 178, 184, 201
addiction, 172–173, 175, 177, 201
attachment style, 21, 201
awareness, 8, 36, 48, 201, 205

B

balance, 31, 78, 104, 121, 144, 165, 184, 201
betrayal, 45, 145, 201, 205
boundaries, 12, 16, 31, 43, 45–46, 55, 59, 64, 78, 91, 93–94, 97, 99, 113–115, 127, 146, 149, 167, 179, 185, 188, 201, 207
business, 67–68, 201

C

career, 24, 28, 52–53, 59, 73, 123, 145, 149, 152–153, 156–157, 163, 201, 208
children, 65, 93, 154, 185, 201
clarity, 7–8, 13, 31, 127, 169, 176, 179, 194, 201
coherence, 12, 67, 77–78, 138, 183–184, 187, 190–194, 199, 201

collapse, 4, 25–26, 34, 64–66, 69–70, 73, 76, 82, 103–104, 107, 120, 124, 127–129, 145, 147–148, 160, 191, 194, 197, 199, 202
compassion, 207
compassion fatigue, 207
competition, 162, 189, 202
conflict, 93, 194, 202
confused, 21, 202
connection, 6, 31, 33, 61, 63, 66, 92, 119, 163–164, 186, 191, 202
contribution, 7, 13–14, 25, 42, 50, 61–66, 69–70, 72–75, 77, 82, 85, 87, 91, 94, 122–130, 134, 136–139, 149, 152–153, 155, 159–166, 184–186, 190, 194, 202, 208
control, 31, 96, 161, 163, 166, 170–171, 188–189, 202, 207
cooperation, 105, 202
crisis, 28, 32, 55, 64–65, 115, 135, 150–153, 157–158, 173–174, 178, 202

D

depleted, 45, 124, 129, 134, 136, 202
depression, 170, 173, 178, 202, 207
discipline, 22–23, 43, 47, 56, 106, 199, 202
disease, 60, 202
drift, 151, 202
drive, 32, 163, 178, 202

E

emdr, 171, 202
excited, 69, 108, 202
exercise, 55, 107, 202, 207
exhaustion, 29, 45, 68, 73, 83, 135, 137, 171, 174, 197, 202

F

failure, 3–5, 8, 12–13, 16–17, 26–28, 43–44, 47–48, 53–56, 58, 64–65, 67, 81, 91, 94, 104–105, 108–109, 111, 122, 126, 138, 144, 152, 155, 158, 161–162, 166, 169, 171, 174–176, 178–179, 186, 199, 202, 207

fear, 26, 31, 76, 202
feedback loop, 6, 11, 21–22, 202
freedom, 53, 155, 165, 202
friend, 37, 65, 89, 94, 96–97, 189, 203

G

grief, 155, 164, 178, 203
grieving, 155, 164, 203
growth, 4–5, 7–8, 13–14, 16–17, 23–26, 28–29, 34, 42, 50–57, 59–60, 63, 66, 70, 72–78, 82–87, 89, 91–95, 103, 113–116, 118–124, 126, 128, 134–139, 144–147, 149–161, 172, 177, 179–180, 184–195, 199, 203
guilt, 50, 76, 83, 185, 203

H

healing, 4, 6, 27, 203
honesty, 7, 15, 46, 137, 192, 203

I

identity, 14, 23–24, 26, 28, 34–35, 42–43, 49, 54–57, 59–60, 65, 72, 75, 77, 82, 85, 89, 92–93, 107, 113–115, 117–118, 120–121, 125, 129, 144–146, 152, 155–157, 161, 185, 189, 191–192, 197, 199, 203, 208
impatience, 15, 87, 203
integration, 12, 70, 72, 78, 133, 140, 203
integrity, 25, 47, 197, 203
intimacy, 93, 203
isolation, 58, 63, 68, 71, 89, 91, 146, 162, 186, 203

L

lead, 36, 73, 203
leadership, 123, 203
loneliness, 162, 203
love, 92, 203

M

manos, 197, 199, 203
marriage, 154–155, 158, 203
mechanic, 6, 32, 170, 203
mentor, 115, 125, 163, 189, 203
mirror, 43, 204
money, 32, 84, 129, 176, 204
muscle, 149, 204

N

narcissistic, 186, 204
nervous system, 33, 42, 47, 56, 90, 97, 105, 170–171, 204

O

obligation, 62, 124–125, 127, 137, 204
operating system, 199, 204
overwhelmed, 52, 90–91, 204

P

parenting, 68, 204
partner, 65, 68, 89, 92, 94, 96–97, 154, 204
pathology, 16, 60, 170, 204
patience, 7, 14, 49, 154, 177, 192, 204
peace, 57, 163, 165, 184, 204
people-pleasing, 45, 204
performance, 34, 36, 42, 47, 54, 72, 160, 188, 199, 204
presence, 64, 125, 164–165, 183, 185–187, 190, 204
pressure, 73, 89, 91, 93, 147, 150, 189, 199, 204
purpose, 4, 26, 33–34, 42, 50, 56, 63, 65–66, 69, 73, 75–77, 85, 87, 91–92, 138, 144, 146, 149, 153, 162, 185–186, 204, 208

R

recovery, 68, 114, 116–117, 137, 149, 172–173, 186, 197, 204, 207
recovery, 68, 114, 116–117, 137, 149, 172–173, 186, 197, 204, 207
regret, 90

relationships, 54–55, 58, 68, 89, 93–99, 117, 146, 154, 156, 163, 178, 191, 204

relief, 56, 74, 204

repair, 6–8, 11–17, 23, 26–27, 31, 34, 36–37, 47–49, 78, 86–99, 101, 103–104, 106, 108, 110–114, 117–118, 120–126, 133, 144, 148, 156, 158, 169–170, 172, 174–175, 177, 179, 192–193, 204

resentful, 85, 129, 204

responsibility, 24–25, 55, 62, 98, 116, 127–128, 148, 205

responsible, 90, 127, 129, 205

restlessness, 46, 205

revenue, 67

rigidity, 138, 205

S

scar tissue, 197, 205

self-awareness, 36, 205

self-betrayal, 45, 205

self-reliance, 178, 205

self-trust, 4–5, 8, 11, 13–17, 23, 25–26, 28, 33, 35, 41–48, 50, 55–56, 59, 62, 70, 72–75, 77–78, 81, 83, 86–87, 89, 91, 103, 106, 109, 111, 134, 144–148, 153, 160, 164, 173–174, 177, 184, 187–188, 191, 205, 207

separation, 114, 117, 205

service, 14, 24–26, 29, 34, 50, 62, 64–66, 69–70, 72, 75–76, 78, 82, 85, 92–93, 122–124, 126–129, 133–134, 136, 138, 149, 160, 162, 174, 186, 194, 205

shame, 8, 12, 16, 23, 34, 36, 46–47, 58, 79, 88, 135, 176, 178, 185, 205

sleep, 22, 44, 55, 58, 105, 107, 115, 188, 190, 205

son, 47

spirituality, 6, 33, 205

standards, 24, 52, 54, 56, 205, 207

strength, 5, 52–53, 164, 205

stress, 86, 205, 207

success, 5, 17, 25, 27–28, 34, 54, 56–57, 62–63, 66–68, 72, 84, 108, 123, 136, 145, 147–148, 152, 171, 197, 205
surrender, 166, 205

T

teenager, 154, 205
tired, 6, 43, 45–47, 68, 135–136, 153, 205
training, 146–147, 177–178, 189, 205
transformation, 7, 14, 103, 106–107, 121, 177, 188, 205
trauma, 3–4, 21, 26, 32, 110, 170–171, 175, 177–178, 205
trust, 4–5, 8, 11, 13–17, 21, 23, 25–26, 28, 33–37, 41–50, 55–56, 59, 62, 66, 70, 72–78, 81–87, 89, 91–92, 94, 103–107, 109–111, 122, 134, 144–148, 153, 160, 164, 173–174, 177, 180, 184, 187–188, 190–191, 205, 207
truth, 37, 47, 65–68, 75, 90, 199, 206

V

values, 59–60, 147–148, 206
vitality, 68, 206
vulnerability, 58, 119, 206

W

wife, 189, 206
wisdom, 24, 57, 64, 68, 82–83, 94, 98, 113, 118, 136, 161, 163, 166, 206
wounds, 4, 6, 30, 32, 206

NOTES

HOW TO USE THIS BOOK

1. Compensatory behaviour is a core concept in self-regulation theory. When a primary regulatory system fails, individuals reliably substitute secondary systems, often maladaptively. See: Carver & Scheier (1998), *On the Self-Regulation of Behavior*.

1. YOU'RE ALREADY RUNNING LOOPS

1. Research in reinforcement learning and behavioural neuroscience consistently shows that durable learning occurs through action–feedback cycles rather than through insight alone. See: Sutton & Barto, *Reinforcement Learning: An Introduction*; and Schultz, Dayan & Montague (1997), "A Neural Substrate of Prediction and Reward," *Science*.
2. Dual-process and embodied cognition research demonstrates that declarative understanding and behavioural change operate through distinct neural systems. See: Kahneman, *Thinking, Fast and Slow*; and Damasio, *The Feeling of What Happens*.
3. Self-trust is strongly associated with self-efficacy and behavioural follow-through. Repeated failure to meet self-set standards measurably reduces perceived self-efficacy, which in turn predicts lower future action rates. See: Bandura (1997), *Self-Efficacy: The Exercise of Control*.
4. Research on caregiver strain/compassion fatigue documents that chronic over-giving without adequate boundaries and recovery is associated with psychological distress and burnout-like symptoms. See: Figley (1995), *Compassion Fatigue: Coping With Secondary Traumatic Stress Disorder in Those Who Treat the Traumatized*.

2. WHY INSIGHT DOESN'T CHANGE ANYTHING

1. Wilson, W. (1939). *Alcoholics Anonymous: The Story of How Many Thousands of Men and Women Have Recovered from Alcoholism*. New York: Works Publishing, p. 289 (from "Bill's Story").

3. LOOP ONE: SELF-TRUST

1. Behavioural activation research shows that small, immediately completable actions produce disproportionate increases in perceived agency and mood, especially in populations experiencing burnout or depression. See: Dimid-

jian et al. (2006), "Behavioral Activation, Cognitive Therapy, and Antidepressant Medication," *Journal of Consulting and Clinical Psychology*.

5. LOOP THREE: MEANING / CONTRIBUTION

1. Longitudinal and population studies have found that having purpose/meaning in life is associated with better health outcomes and lower mortality risk, suggesting that "meaning" is not just philosophy but a measurable factor tied to wellbeing. See: Alimujiang et al. (2019), "Association Between Life Purpose and Mortality," *JAMA Network Open*.

6. HOW THE LOOPS INTERACT

1. Work-identity fusion is a documented predictor of burnout, relational strain, and depressive symptoms. See: Schaufeli, Leiter & Maslach (2009), "Burnout: 35 years of research and practice," *Career Development International*.

8. RELATIONAL LOOPS

1. Avoidance masked as value-driven choice is a known cognitive defence pattern. Acceptance and Commitment Therapy literature describes this as "experiential avoidance." See: Hayes, Strosahl & Wilson, *Acceptance and Commitment Therapy*.

15. LOOPS AT 60 AND BEYOND

1. Adult development research shows that wellbeing in midlife and later adulthood depends on shifting from acquisition and achievement goals toward generativity, contribution, and transmission. See: Erikson, *Identity and the Life Cycle*; and Lachman (2015), "Mind the Gap in the Middle," *Psychological Science in the Public Interest*.

16. WHEN THIS BOOK ISN'T ENOUGH

1. Clinical psychology distinguishes between structural self-regulation problems and psychopathology. Frameworks like this are effective for the former but insufficient for the latter, where specialised clinical intervention is required. See: Insel (2009), "Disruptive Insights in Psychiatry," *Nature*.

www.ingramcontent.com/pod-product-compliance
Lightning Source LLC
Chambersburg PA
CBHW071343080526
44587CB00017B/2939